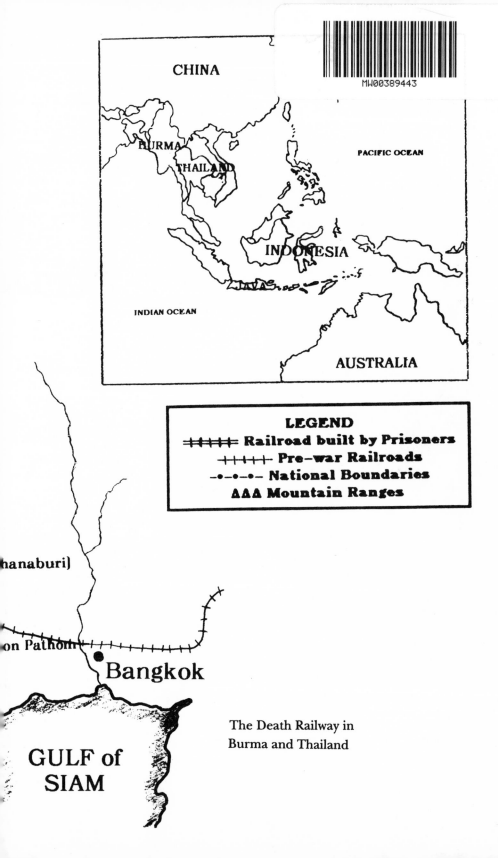

CHINA

PACIFIC OCEAN

BURMA

THAILAND

INDONESIA

JAVA

INDIAN OCEAN

AUSTRALIA

MW00389443

LEGEND
┼┼┼┼┼ Railroad built by Prisoners
┼┼┼┼┼ Pre-war Railroads
–•–•–•– National Boundaries
▲▲▲ Mountain Ranges

hanaburi]

on Pathom

● Bangkok

GULF of
SIAM

The Death Railway in
Burma and Thailand

A Thousand Cups of Rice

Surviving The Death Railway

KYLE THOMPSON

Member of the "Lost Battalion"

EAKIN PRESS ★ Austin, Texas

FIRST EDITION

Copyright © 1994
By Kyle Thompson

Published in the United States of America
By Eakin Press
An Imprint of Sunbelt Media, Inc.
P.O. Drawer 90159 ★ Austin, TX 78709-0159

ISBN 0-89015-990-4

2   3   4   5   6   7   8   9   10

Library of Congress Cataloging-in-Publication Data

Thompson, Kyle, 1922–
    A thousand cups of rice : surviving the Death Railway / Kyle Thompson.
        p.   cm.
    Includes bibliographical references and index.
    ISBN 0-89015-990-4 : $19.95
    1. Thompson, Kyle, 1922-. 2. World War, 1939–1945 — Prisoners and prisons, Japanese. 3. World War, 1939–1945 — Concentration camps — Burma — Personal narraties, American. 4. World War, 1939–1945 — Personal narratives, American. 5. Prisoners of war — Burma — Biography. 6. Prisoners of war — United States — Biography. 7. Burma–Siam Railroad. I. Title. D805.B9T46   1994
940.54'7252'09591–dc20   94-22388
                                                                      CIP

Dedicated to those men of the
Lost Battalion Association;
The 2d Battalion, 131st Field Artillery Regiment
of the 36th Division, Texas National Guard, and
the USS *Houston* (CA-30)
Who died in combat and in Japanese prisoner of war camps.
Three artillerymen and 792 members of the *Houston*'s crew
Died in battle before capture, March 8, 1942.
Nine hundred four soldiers, sailors,
and Marines were imprisoned.
One hundred sixty-six died of hunger, disease,
and physical abuse.

I am standing on the seashore.
A ship spreads her white sails to the morning breeze and starts for the
ocean. I stand watching her until she fades on the horizon, and
someone at my side says, "She is gone."
Gone where? The loss of sight is in me, not in her.
Just at the moment when someone says, "She is gone," there are others
who are watching her coming. Other voices take up the glad shout,
*"Here she comes," and **that** is dying.*
— Henry Scott Holland

Contents

The War

The war is very dangeris. There are bombs misils and tanks.

My grandfather was in world war 2. so was my grandpaw but he flew a plane in the war.

When my grandfather was here he told me, my mom, my dad, my grandmother and my sister about the war. he said that all he got to eat was 1 cup of brown rice a day.

One other thing he told us about is that the japanese forts were made out of leaves. he also told me he went up to one of the Japanese and asked for some medicine. He also had to build a rail road. About evry thing he did was work.

I forgot hoo answered the door.

he rode about 5 trains. he did not by a ticket. he had to risk his life and jump on. when his mother found out he was alive and saw him she almost fanted because he was alive and back.

The End

Colin Andrew Montgomery
The author's grandson
Age 6

Acknowledgments

This is a personal account of how a teenage American soldier survived inhuman mental and physical stress as one of hundreds of thousands of Allied prisoners of war and Asian coolie laborers who built the infamous Death Railway in Burma and Thailand during World War II.

It is written specifically for, and is dedicated to my beloved wife, Vivian Carter Thompson, our daughters, Linda Sue (Mrs. David) Montgomery, Thelma Kay Thompson, and Janis Kyle Thompson; and to our two grandchildren, Alice Amanda Montgomery and Colin Andrew Montgomery, who suggested the title of this book. I wanted all of them to know a little of what it was like then.

This volume originally was intended as a private report to my family, and perhaps for a few friends. However, over a period of three or four years, it developed to the extent that some thought was given to publication. It would not have been published, though, without the strong support and encouragement of my wife, Vivian. I am especially indebted to her for her tireless work on endless details from editing to hand addressing hundreds of brochures announcing the publication.

I also acknowledge the work done by my editor, Jeffrey E. Phillips, whose knowledge and insight were invaluable. Phillips, an author himself, recently wrote *America's First Team in the Gulf,* the history of the 1st Cavalry Division in the war against Iraq, published by Taylor Publishing Co., Dallas.

My special thanks also go to Jess H. Stanbrough of Falmouth, Massachusetts, who I consider my mentor during my soldier years, 1940–1945, Jo Ellen Hewins, a bright young Corpus Christi attorney and a special friend, and daughters Linda, Kay, and Janis for their help in editing these pages and shaping this story.

– KYLE THOMPSON

A Thousand Cups of Rice

Surviving The Death Railway

Member of the "Lost Battalion"

1.

In the Beginning

DENSE, WATER-LADEN CLOUDS dumped a near solid blanket of water over the thick forest. A dull roar, like a long line of waterfalls, heralded the maturity of the tropical monsoon. Frail, weary figures, most of them naked except for the filthy g-strings barely covering their crotches, struggled as if in slow motion through mud and muck. Over the roar of the torrent rose the shrill voice of Japanese army guards yelling, *"Speedo! Speedo!"*

Deep in the Burma jungles, 105 kilometers from the coastal town of Thanbyuzayat, the diseased and starving slave-workers bent to their labors, nearer death than life. Among them was a contingent of the 131st Field Artillery Regiment, some 550 men of the regiment's 2d Battalion, who had been detached from the 36th Division, Texas National Guard, late in 1941. The artillerymen struggled alongside survivors of the sunken heavy cruiser USS *Houston*. As fighting men of a world power, they were unrecognizable. Their war was over; they fought now merely to survive another hour, another minute.

The artillery battalion's original destination had been the Philippines, but the Imperial Japanese Navy changed these plans when it launched its unprovoked sneak attack on Pearl Harbor, December 7, 1941, plunging the United States into the Second World War.

Given their choice, Burma is perhaps the last place in the

1

world to which this handful of prisoners of war would have come. It lies along the belly of Asia, the world's largest and most diverse continent, containing three-fifths of the earth's land area. Few, if any, of the Americans had ever given this Texas-size mass on the Southeast Asia map more than a glance in a high school geography class. Now, minds dulled with exhaustion, none looked on this part of the Asian continent with any romanticism, although the monsoons might have reminded them that the vast region fed some of the world's greatest, most historic rivers: the Tigris and the Euphrates, the Indus, the Ganges, the Brahmaputra, and Burma's own Irrawaddy.

Burma's tropical climate is heavily influenced by the monsoons of southern Asia. This part of the world has three seasons: the cool, dry period running from October to February; a hot, dry season that lasts from early March to mid-May; and the monsoon that starts gradually in late May, crescendos in June, July, and August, then fades away by late September.

The monsoon dumps up to two hundred inches of rain annually along the coastal plains and one hundred inches in the delta. Forests carpet half of Burma. The delta region contains lush mangrove stands while the rain forests are thick with hardwoods that include a plentiful supply of teak. Under the rain forest canopy live a variety of game birds, elephant, and tiger. It is a place of abundant life.

The staple diet in Burma is rice and fish. Three-quarters of the population live in the vast Irrawaddy River valley and along the coastal strips. However, there was in 1942 not so much as a small village, not even a single bamboo hut located in the dense jungles 105 kilometers south of Thanbyuzayat. We were intruders in the rain forests, most of us physically and mentally beyond the breaking point. The only real evidence of human habitation in this lonely jungle was an occasional split bamboo platform about six feet by six feet, raised three feet from the ground, where an unfortunate Burmese victim of leprosy was dumped in isolation to live out the remaining days of his life. To stumble upon one of these hapless victims recalls scenes from movies depicting mobs, during the days when Christ was on earth, yelling "Unclean! Unclean!"

Deep in the Burma jungle, the monsoon peaked. Rain fell unendingly day in and day out. The world was water, mud, disease, and misery. We were about midway into the task of building a 260-mile railroad through virgin jungles from near Moulmein, Burma, to Kanchanaburi, Thailand. The British, who had held Burma as part of their colonial empire since 1885, had surveyed the same area in the 1930s and abandoned plans to build a rail line there as impractical at best, impossible at worst.

The Japanese were desperate to complete the railroad, however, since it was essential to keep a steady flow of war materials moving through Thailand to its army in northern Burma. The only links in that area relied on the long and exposed sea route to Rangoon by way of Singapore and the Strait of Malacca, and a primitive road winding through southern Burma that was unfit for prolonged heavy traffic, as it was little more than a dirt road used mainly by oxen-drawn carts.

When Singapore fell on February 15, 1942, the Japanese captured more than 130,000 troops of the British Empire, including nearly 68,000 colonial soldiers from India. Many of these, along with the handful of Americans and the remnants of the Dutch army captured when Java fell on March 8, 1942, were to be the nucleus of workers destined to become slave laborers on the infamous "Death Railway."

Thousands of these prisoners were jammed into holds of grimy, ancient Japanese cargo ships like the British collier sold to the Japanese in the 1920s and renamed the *Dai Nichi Maru*. Others were wedged into metal boxcars or were forced to march for hundreds of miles as Nippon herded them toward Burma and Thailand in late 1942 and early 1943 to join the "Burma railroad gang." It has been estimated that 330,000 workers, including 61,000 prisoners of war, were employed on the railroad.

It was a monumental task — one considered impossible by Western standards. But our captors were approaching it from the Asian perspective, and more specifically, with standards applied by the Japanese Imperial Army.

The magnitude of the task, and the degree of suffering facing the Allied prisoners and the estimated 270,000 coolie laborers recruited from throughout Southeast Asia, is made clear by some of the railroad statistics supplied jointly by Japanese records and Allied documents: Japanese engineers stated that to complete the railroad bed itself would involve the building of 4 million cubic meters of earthwork, distributing 3 million cubic meters of rock, and constructing fourteen kilometers (eight and one-half miles) of bridgework in a period of less than one year. The tools they provided were picks, sledgehammers, shovels, and bamboo baskets.

Our horde of Allied prisoners and Asian conscript laborers plunged into this herculean task early in 1943, largely ignorant of what was facing us; emaciated, sick, beaten, we were driven relentlessly amid the rock and mud and fetid swamp for eighteen or more hours each day. Completion of the railroad bed, along with its cuts, fills, and bridges, inched along into the jungles at a pace semi-satisfactory to the Japanese until the monsoon began to take its toll both on humans and materials. As the monsoon built toward its climactic crescendo in mid-1943, we began to fall behind. Our Japanese masters increased the work load in a desperate effort to catch up. Food, which had been inadequate to sustain normal activity, became even scarcer. The rains began to wash out roads and some makeshift bridges used to truck supplies to the work sites.

A few weeks earlier I had been part of a crew working back down the line near the 80 Kilo Camp, which lay eighty kilometers from the railroad's origin at Thanbyuzayat. We were constructing a double-deck bridge across a moderately wide river. One of the huge timbers being used as bridge piling slipped and scuffed my right leg in two places midway between the knee and ankle. I washed the small wounds with river water, and continued working with hardly a break.

Within a couple of days, the two bruises became infected. They turned into a pair of round, black, open sores, each about the size of a nickel. For several weeks, these wounds remained docile — two little black sores waiting to blossom into tropical ulcers.

Our group, known as Burma Railroad Party Branch 5, under command of our own Lt. Col. Blutcher S. Tharp, the 2d Battalion commander, had begun work on the line late in January 1943.

On March 15, we were trucked past the Branch 3 work party, consisting mostly of British prisoners, to 85 Kilo Camp. After spending two weeks building bamboo huts to hold a normal camp contingent of some five thousand POWs, we hoisted our gear on our backs and marched five kilometers back to 80 Kilo Camp, which was to be our home for the next two months.

Our brief interlude at 80 Kilo Camp soon passed, although I did not then realize that within weeks I would be returning to face one of the most horrible experiences of my life. The railroad bed had been completed far enough into the jungles so that by the end of May we left 80 Kilo and marched through a steady rain, carrying all our worldly belongings, twenty kilometers deeper into the jungles to the infamous 100 Kilo Camp.

Meantime, our physical strength steadily deteriorated from a lack of food and continuous attacks of malaria, dysentery, and other diseases. Our efforts hampered by the eternal monsoon, we fell critically behind in our work quota. The Japanese accelerated the pace, the guards cried *"Speedo, Speedo,"* and we began working a full eighteen hours daily. We had been in this misery for three weeks when my two leg wounds suddenly began to widen and deepen. Within days, my leg was a solid mass of black, rotting flesh, and pus — a full-blown tropical ulcer stretching from the knee to the ankle. The bone was exposed at the site of each original wound.

My agonies were not unique. In addition to the tropical ulcers, most of us were chronically plagued with attacks of malaria about once every three weeks, while some suffered from dysentery and from various forms of malnutrition that included pellagra and beriberi.

Already in a weakened condition from overwork and undernourishment, what little strength I had soon departed me. My ulcerated leg was a mess. In a matter of days, I could not stand upright, and had to keep the leg elevated to prevent it from leaking my life away in a steady stream of blood.

Soon I was added to the growing list of useless baggage in a work camp. I thus became eligible for passage back to 80 Kilo, where the Japanese had established a so-called "hospital camp." I didn't realize it at the time, but this was where prisoners unable to work were sent to die.

This was the low point of my POW existence. I was in the world of the dead and dying. It became much easier to die than to live. I had celebrated my twenty-first birthday a few weeks before, with odds heavily in favor of my never reaching number twenty-two. The events of the past couple of years began floating through my mind, and I started to dream of home with its hamburgers, Tom Mix movies and, what now was obvious, the good life we had left behind.

2.

Dark War Clouds

THE DARK CLOUDS of war hanging over distant Europe made little impression on my teenage contemporaries back in Wichita Falls, Texas, in the summer of 1940. It was my senior year, but I foolishly dropped out of high school in early spring just three months short of graduation. I was having some trouble with an advanced algebra class, so I just decided to quit — to toss in the old towel. My father was not too much on school anyway, and he welcomed the fact that I had obtained a job as a swamper on a city milk delivery truck, and could contribute about five dollars each week to help with household expenses.

Because they did not affect us in America, Hitler's overrunning of first Poland in late 1939, then Denmark, Sweden, Holland, Finland, and finally France, drew scant notice among my circle of friends as did the heroic efforts in the summer of 1940 by the British to evacuate hundreds of thousands of Allied troops from Dunkirk. We could not know that a couple of years later we would be thrown together with some of those same English evacuees in prisoner of war camps throughout Southeast Asia.

But that was still in the future, and at hand was the eventful summer of 1940. My best buddy at the time was a neighbor my age named Ruel Marvin, a handsome guy who consequently seemed to have more success with the girls. He was a messenger boy for Western Union, a much more sophisticated profession than my job on the milk truck. I usually worked seven days a week for my dollar-a-day salary. Ruel, on the other hand, would work only four or five days weekly and made more than that in tips.

Our jobs left us little leisure time, but what time we could muster often found us lounging around Ruel's house (his parents worked) and talking about girls. I had a crush on a girl named Bobby Banks, but never actually dated her. She seemed always to play hard-to-get with me, and I knew it, but nonetheless swooned over my secret love. Later, when the army called, whatever secret attraction she may have commanded faded against the prospects of this exciting new life — the first time in my eighteen years of existence that I would be on my own, away from home.

I was infatuated with the big band music then in vogue. My all-time favorite radio program (this was long before television) was "Your Hit Parade." As I recall, the Hit Parade was broadcast on Monday nights, and I waited with great anticipation to find out the week's top ten hits. I lived for Tommy Dorsey, Glenn Miller, Benny Goodman, and a dozen similar groups that could leave you dancing all night. Their music included "Till The End of Time," "I Don't Know Why I Love You Like I Do," "Sentimental Journey," "Chattanooga Choo Choo," "The Gypsy," "If I Didn't Care," "We Three," "My Prayer," and many, many more. The big band music of the 1930s and 1940s is still my favorite, although the young people of today often refer to it as "elevator music."

I had joined the Texas National Guard early in 1938, although at sixteen I was underage. I talked my mother into signing papers showing my age to be eighteen, and qualified. Nevertheless, I recall old Sergeant Davis, the full-time advisor assigned to our regiment, grumbling under his breath, "That kid's not a day over sixteen." I was furious. I was more than two hundred days over sixteen!

The few dollars paid to us for the weekly drills, plus extra pay for summer camp, came in handy. We still were in the grip of the dreadful depression of the 1930s, and a few bucks went a long way. Our two-week camp in 1940 was spent at Camp Hulen, Palacios, on the Texas Gulf Coast. It was my first experience with saltwater, and the few times we were able to go to the beach I thoroughly enjoyed.

The trip to the Gulf Coast was perhaps my first exposure to the wonders of the world outside my own family home. Our convoy left Wichita Falls and headed south on a four hundred-mile ride that revealed to me the marvels and the greatness of Texas. Until this trip, my world had consisted of farming in Montague County, the "big" city of Wichita Falls, three or four family excursions at Christmas to Emmet, Arkansas, and one expedition with a friend my age to faraway Lawton, Oklahoma.

One memorable event during the trip to Palacios was dinner at The Raven, a large restaurant in Huntsville, Texas. It was an impressive establishment, with a dining room big enough to accommodate our Headquarters Battery group of just over one hundred. Uniformed waitresses — at least a half-dozen — scurried about, attending a hundred ravenous appetites momentarily freed from the shackles of army chow halls and army chow. I had never been served a meal in such elegant surroundings. I was only a few weeks away from my eighteenth birthday!

Summer merged into fall and the war in Europe worsened. President Franklin D. Roosevelt was attempting to do what he could to help beleaguered England, the only barrier left between Hitler and world domination. Congress was heavily isolationist, but Roosevelt finally persuaded that august body to go along with legislation to mobilize the National Guard and Army Reserves.

I was a buck private, an apprentice Morse code radio operator in Regimental Headquarters Battery, 131st Field Artillery of the Texas National Guard 36th Division. Our unit was made up of some one hundred men, all from the Wichita Falls area. Commanding this battery was Capt. Winthrop H. Rogers, who owned and operated an automobile service station. Second in command was 1st Lt. Marvin M. Rudd, an accountant with the Internal Revenue Service.

We were called to active duty on November 25, 1940, and were immediately housed in the Bailey Moline Hardware store, a vacant two-story building in downtown Wichita Falls at 10th and Indiana streets. I started out in the regular Army at twenty-one dollars a month, but moved up the ladder to thirty dollars within three months, which was about the length of time we stayed in the downtown building, mostly loafing around in our bunks. Fortunately, there was no open space in the area for our superiors to put us through close order drills and a lot of other useless things soldiers do to keep out of mischief.

Meanwhile, building contractors were busy throwing together a tent city at the newly named Camp Bowie at Brownwood, one hundred miles southwest of Wichita Falls. It was mid-January when we arrived at Camp Bowie, our home for most of the remainder of 1941. Construction was still going on when we arrived at the camp. There were few paved streets and no sidewalks. Most of the buildings to house our trucks and equipment had been completed, and there were plenty of wooden frames for the one-hundred-square-foot tents that housed eight men, and were to be our home away from home for the next eleven months.

This was a new and exciting world for most of us. I was eighteen — finally a legitimate age for the army — and it was my initial experience of living away from my family. I had begun accumulating a list of new friends, many of whom would end up being closer to me than my blood relations. Among these new "brothers" were Wilson G. "Dub" Reed, Jr., H. A. Kitchings, and Frank Faulkner, all Wichita Falls boys about my age.

Actually, Reed was the youngest of the four — he was only sixteen when we became prisoners of war some fourteen months later. Dub and I became instant friends, probably because I still was somewhat immature for my age and Reed, at about fourteen, was already full of life and approached it with a smirk on his face and friendly, happy eyes that missed little of what was going on around him.

All of us except Kitchings were members of a nine-man radio section in Regimental Headquarters Battery. Our section leader was S.Sgt. Jess H. Stanbrough. It was our responsibility to coordinate communications for the regiment which consisted of two battalions of field artillery, a service battery whose members took care of all our mechanical needs, and a medical detachment to handle our physical health. Our mental well-being was up to us. Each of the field artillery battalions had three batteries, with a total of about 550 men. A regimental band performed daily to mark the end of the day as we assembled on the road that dissected our living area.

After settling down in our new camp quarters, the serious business of making professional soldiers of a collection of school boys began in earnest. We set up a school to learn the Morse code. One was considered a journeyman when he could muster eighteen words per minute. Reed and I seemed to take to the code naturally, and under the able tutelage of Sergeant Stanbrough, we soon were designated chief radio operators for the regiment.

After advancing in pay past the thirty-dollar-per-month category in early spring, 1941, I bought my very first automobile. What teenager doesn't vividly remember his or her first car? It was a 1934 Chevrolet four-door sedan. I paid a hefty $125 for it, buying it on credit when my dad agreed to co-sign the loan. My old Chevy turned out to be something of a lemon. The motor had bad rods, the previous owner having put heavy-duty oil in the crankshaft to keep the knocking silent long enough for me to sign the papers and drive it away.

One weekend when I was on KP, some of my friends talked me into lending them the Chevy so they could go home to Wichita Falls. I failed to tell them that they had to check the oil every few miles, and as was to be expected, they burned out the rods before the weekend was over. We later had the car towed into Brownwood where a local garage owner agreed to overhaul the motor. I think he charged me seventy-five dollars, although I was only able to pay five dollars down, hoping to get the remainder to him at a clip of five dollars per month. I don't recall ever having paid all of that bill.

As soon as the old Chevy was running again, I got back to Wichita Falls and traded it in on a 1938 Ford. At last I was somebody with decent wheels. It was only about three years old, cost a hefty three hundred dollars and ran like a top!

Meanwhile, Wiley Wisdom, who had become our mess sergeant after we arrived at Camp Bowie, was promoted to first sergeant. This turned out to be bad news for Reed and me. For some reason, we jointly earned the top listing on his detail "hit" list. Wisdom did everything he could to get both of us on every dirty detail that came up. Kitchen police, or KP, was the worst job in the camp. Wisdom delighted in putting either or both of us on KP whenever possible. The problem was that we were exempt from all work details during the week, but not on Saturdays and Sundays. It isn't difficult to guess where Reed and I spent most of our weekends.

Sergeant Wisdom's ascension to power in the mess hall followed the brief, ignominious reign of an NCO who shall remain nameless. Some of our group had begun to suspect that this sergeant was responsible for the disappearance of a lot of our better-grade foods, so they conspired to set up a trap. One person hid among the garbage cans at the back of the kitchen with a camera to keep watch. The vigilance soon paid off. The good sergeant was seen loading full hams and some canned goods into the trunk of his car parked at the curb.

The person with the camera clicked away, and these photographs were developed and mailed anonymously to Col. Thomas A. Bay, our regimental commander. In short order, the sergeant was court-martialed and given a dishonorable discharge. It was at this time that Wisdom moved in as chief of the kitchen staff.

Wisdom looked the part of a mess sergeant. He was a heavy man with beady eyes peering out of a large, oval face with flabby jaws. His midsection bulged over both sides of his belt, probably from over-sampling the starchy army meals he prepared for us. Even after he moved out of the kitchen and took over as top sergeant, he continued his keen interest in the affairs of the mess hall.

A few months after our arrival at Camp Bowie, I had been promoted to private first class, third class specialist — a rank that somehow disappeared during the war. But I was making a whopping sixty-eight dollars a month, a real fortune. Even this great sum of money seemed somehow to fall short before the month ended. This is where our loan shark of a first sergeant would ride forth to the rescue.

Wisdom operated an open lending venture out of the headquarters tent. He would lend anyone in our battery up to twenty dollars, but the interest was, to put it mildly, appalling. If you could repay the loan during the first two weeks of the month, the interest was only 25 percent. The third week of the month saw the interest soar to 50 percent, but if you let the loan run the full month, interest swelled to 100 percent. In other words, if you borrowed five dollars and waited the full month, you owed him ten dollars. And Wisdom had a sure method of collection. As first sergeant, he presided over payday. He would place a table outside the headquarters tent and we would line up for our monthly pay. As you approached the table, Wisdom would take out his little ledger and say, "Let's see, Thompson. You borrowed five dollars from me on June 5; you now owe me ten dollars," and he would deduct the ten dollars and hand you the remainder of your pay. He must have been wealthy before we left Camp Bowie that November!

The summer of 1941 saw us pack all our gear, load up in our trucks, and head for the swamps and pine forests of Louisiana for the great sham battle in the Louisiana Maneuvers. First Sergeant Wisdom made good use of Reed and me during these training exercises. Our unit was constantly on the move, but when we reached a site where it appeared we might stay for a time, Wisdom hit the ground yelling: "Reed! Thompson! Front and center!" We rushed up, stood at attention, and he pointed to the supply truck. "Grab a pick and shovel and start digging."

We knew what was in store. We started digging a six-by-six-by-six-foot garbage hole. If we were in the same location long enough, we also had to dig a deep trench for a latrine. The latter hole only had to be three-by-six-by-six feet. But often we hit the trucks and moved again before, or just after we finished the first ditch.

The Louisiana woods was home to feral hogs, and during one of our brief stops, Sgt. Wilburn Rockett managed to corner and capture one only a few weeks old. Wilburn kept the small, black pig and soon the animal followed him about like a puppy. He kept his pet for several months, finally having to dispose of it when we were ordered overseas toward the end of 1941.

To our everlasting relief, the Louisiana Maneuvers soon ended and we were back in our good old tents at Camp Bowie. Our radio section resumed its radio training operations. We settled into our camp routines, some of us going home for weekends and others again winding up on kitchen police duty.

On one of those weekends, Sgt. Frank W. Ficklin, whose family lived next door to my then-future wife in Wichita Falls, was assigned orderly duty. This meant he had to stay in camp as the noncommissioned duty officer. One of our group, Cpl. James G. Alexander, was a few years older that most of the lower ranks, but was well-known by everybody. Jimmy, as he was commonly addressed, was one of the funniest, brightest, and most well-liked persons in our unit. He also liked to drink, and nearly every weekend would come back off leave well into his cups. It was in this condition that he approached Ficklin on a Saturday afternoon and said, "What are you doing, Fick?"

"I'm listening to a football game," Ficklin replied.

"Who's playing?" Jimmy asked.

"The University of New Mexico and Texas School of Mines."

"Hell, Texas doesn't have any mines," Alexander shot back. There was a brief pause, then he continued. "What's the score?"

"I don't know," Ficklin said.

"Idaho, hell! I thought you told me Texas was playing a while ago!"

As the summer of 1941 progressed, we became more aware that the situation in Europe was steadily growing bleaker. We were, however, less aware of the growing tension in the Far East between the United States and Japan.

In 1937 Japan had invaded China, marking a sharp downturn in relations between the U.S. and the Japanese. America was in a good position to put pressure on Japan because the Japanese economy depended almost exclusively on imported raw materials. Shortly after the invasion of China, the U.S. placed an embargo on the sale of strategic goods to Japan, moving the two countries closer to hostilities.

The world moved to the brink of war when, on September 27, 1940, Japan formally joined the Axis powers made up of Germany and Italy. By this time, virtually all of Europe lay under the domination of Adolf Hitler and his lesser ally, Italian dictator Benito Mussolini. It must have appeared to the Japanese a prudent move to ally themselves with the Axis as Hitler was master of most of Europe. The pact stipulated that the three nations would come to the aid of one another should any one of them be attacked "by a power not involved in the European war." This phrase was obviously designed to intimidate the United States and hopefully keep the powerful U.S. Navy in the Pacific at bay.

Japan expanded its Asiatic war on July 24, 1941, by invading Indochina (now Vietnam). President Roosevelt clamped a trade embargo on Japan and froze its assets in America. This act effectively paralyzed Japan financially, and threatened to leave her war machine inoperative within eighteen months.

The Japanese military, now under the domination of a militant group headed by the dictatorial Gen. Hideki Tojo, activated secret plans in Tokyo that called for expansion southward all the way to Australia. Their most immediate target was the occupation of what was then known as the Netherlands East Indies and the vast mineral resources Japan needed for its existence. It was this specific move that would have such a profound effect on the destiny of the small group of Texans in the 2d Battalion, 131st Field Artillery Regiment.

A few weeks after our division returned from Louisiana that summer, the Pentagon decided that the entire U.S. Army, still organized on the basis of World War I experience, must be reorganized to meet the new threat.

The 36th Division had grown to its full strength of nearly 30,000 men. Military experts determined that such divisions were too cumbersome and ordered a major overhaul. To streamline our division, some of its unwieldy size had to be whittled away. One part of the plan called for the 2d Battalion, 131st Field Artillery Regiment, to be "surplused" and detached. The remaining units of the regiment, including our original Regimental Headquarters Battery, underwent a major overhaul. Most of the old headquarters unit was transferred intact into Headquarters Battery, 2d Battalion, a group that had been stationed in Decatur before mobilization.

We were given several days' leave to go home and bid farewell to family and friends, since our new unit was soon to be shipped out. I returned home to Wichita Falls, where I left my trusty '38 Ford in the care of my father. For some reason, the few days' leave passed in a strange and artificial atmosphere. Both we and our families seemed to sense that something was coming to forever change our lives. We intuitively knew that the 2d Battalion was headed into dangerous waters, but none had even a hint of just what we were facing.

After returning to Camp Bowie for the last time, on November 11, 1941, we loaded ourselves and our equipment on a troop train and headed west, leaving Texas under secret orders with our destination known only by the code name "Plum." I was too naive to realize it at the time, but the twilight of my youth was slipping away. We were headed blindly and inadequately equipped into war. Our newly issued 37mm antitank guns bore silent witness to our unreadiness, making the journey to Java without any ammunition.

It was my very first train trip, and our West Coast destination was by far my most distant excursion away from home. We had real Pullman berths, and holding the rank of only private first class, I naturally was relegated to the upper bunk. That, however, did nothing to dampen my excitement at traveling the overland trail through Texas, New Mexico, Arizona, and California.

We would stop periodically on the way westward and load sack lunches, since we lacked the luxury of dining cars. The food, however, was something of an improvement over some of the slop Wisdom and his kitchen crew served us back in Camp Bowie.

3.

Off to War

SAN FRANCISCO! Whata romantic place for a group of small-town Texans, many of whom had never been more than a few hundred miles from home. We left our troop train and boarded ferries to cross San Francisco Bay for Angel Island, a gathering place for troops destined for overseas duty in the Pacific. Our eyes widened and mouths gaped as our boat passed infamous Alcatraz, America's most notorious prison and subject of countless Hollywood movies.

Although we were in San Francisco fewer than ten days, we still managed a few hours of leave. We rode the trolleys uphill and down, and ate Chinese food in famous Chinatown. Most of us were fascinated with Market Street and its fabulous shops, along with those inviting little step-down bars. Stanbrough recalled how he, Wisdom, and Sgt. Herschel Cobb took in their first burlesque show, a strip joint in the international settlement.

"Wisdom soon tired of the show, saying they all looked the same and besides, it was time to go back to the base," Stanbrough said. "We all agreed and back to Angel Island we went."

On November 21, we gorged on the most fabulous Thanksgiving dinner most of us had ever seen. What a feast that was.

"They must be fattening us up for the kill," Reed told me after we had stuffed ourselves on turkey and dressing with all the trimmings.

The following day, November 22, we took ferry boats to the San Francisco waterfront and marched down the docks and aboard the USS *Republic,* a 28,000-ton troop transport that had once served the German navy as the *Kaiser Wilhelm.* Built in 1904, it was confiscated by the United States in World War I.

We passed under the Golden Gate Bridge and eased into the Pacific Ocean. A new world lay ahead of us. It was with mixed feelings and a great deal of excitement that we hung over the rails of the *Republic* and watched the skyline of San Francisco grow smaller. As we emerged from beneath the Golden Gate Bridge and headed to the southwest, the greying shoreline gradually receded and disappeared. Before we realized it, the vast Pacific had embraced us.

Our thirty-day crossing was to be on calm seas, but first we experienced a misery familiar to most passengers on board a cramped transport ship.

Just off the West Coast the sea can be most deceptive. The water there rolls relentlessly toward land, creating large ground swells. Such was the case as we got out to sea on our first day on board. The *Republic* began to heave slowly up and down, up and down. After settling into our bunk area, most of us were anxious to explore this new marvel of a floating hotel. However, the constant heaving and swaying of the big ship soon took effect, and a good share of the five thousand troops on the *Republic* became violently seasick.

I had made my way to the very top — an area known as the sun deck — to catch as much of the sights as possible, unaware that this was the worst place to be. The swells became more pronounced, and the *Republic* began to sway like a cork in a rippling stream. As the afternoon wore on, more and more soldiers became ill; they tossed their cookies at every point on the ship. There was vomit on the stairways, at water fountains, in the toilets, and virtually everywhere. My head began to swim, and I realized that I had not eaten all day due to the excitement of shipping out.

Getting dizzier and dizzier, I started making my way down several flights of stairs, looking for the dining hall, thinking that some food in my stomach might drive the dizziness away. Just before the galley entrance, a water fountain on the left side virtually overflowed with vomit. That almost finished me, but finally I reached the kitchen and opened the double-hinged doors. A cloud of steam laced with the stench of fish hit me full in the face. It was Friday, and naturally, the navy cooks were serving fish. It must have been fish abandoned by the Germans in the First World War. I was overwhelmed. Everything I had eaten during the past several days surged back up my throat. I dashed to the nearest open door and onto a deck, barely reaching the rail before it all came up and cascaded into the silently malevolent Pacific. Making my way to my hammock, I threw myself into it and stayed there for the next twelve hours.

By the following day I had recovered sufficiently to get down some breakfast. Most of us recovered in short order and made the remainder of the trip across the Pacific in good shape, but not all of us. One of our group, who shall remain anonymous, had bragged endlessly of his many trips around the world as we were preparing to embark in San Francisco. He convinced most of us that he had traveled the seven seas and was a seasoned sailor. Much of his braggadocio, however, disappeared after that first day aboard the *Republic*. He became violently seasick and remained hospitalized until our arrival in Australia nearly a month later.

It took us about a week to reach Hawaii, finally rounding Diamond Head and docking in Pearl Harbor on Saturday, November 29. Most of us got a three-hour pass and wandered through the streets of Honolulu, acting like kids at a circus. But with Pearl Harbor's devastation and war still a week in the future, the Hawaiian Islands were already in a state of wartime alertness. On the following day, we moved out to sea at sunrise, noting that the big fleet of ships that had been there the day before had disappeared. As we pulled further away we were joined by four other transports, and later that day the cruiser USS *Pensacola* took her place at the head of our convoy and remained with us until we arrived safely at Brisbane, Australia.

Destination "Plum" was soon exposed to us as the Philippine Islands, and toward them our convoy set a course generally westward. The next several days passed with most of us getting our sea legs and learning our way around the *Republic*, which was something like a twelve-story floating hotel, albeit a reeking one at the outset. Most of us smoked and once we got away from land, tax-free cigarettes earned five cents a pack for the major brands, and three cents for others. Poker proved a favorite game to pass the time. One day we had a hot game going and I picked up a royal flush on the first draw. Trying to hide my excitement, I opened for one dollar, not unusually high for an opening bet in that game. All five of my opponents threw in their hand, and my prowess as a poker player was established for eternity, although I never was actually accused of having a poker face.

Soon our convoy approached the equator in the vicinity of the Gilbert Islands and the navy crew aboard the *Republic* prepared to initiate us into the "mysterious realm of Neptune Rex." We were forced to crawl through canvas wind tunnels while being sprayed with high-pressure hoses of sea water, made to sit in an electrified "barber chair" and be dunked in a vat of sea water after having barber shears passed through our hair, or in some cases, suffer having half a mustache cut away, all the while being generally harassed by our tormentors, who had already been initiated into Neptune's realm. The barber's chair must have been especially made for this ceremony. It was a massive piece of furniture made of one-by-four strips of lumber and mounted on a platform adjacent to the vat of sea water. The rear legs were attached to the platform by hinges so it could be pushed backward, dumping the occupant into the water.

On December 7, 1941, our commanding officer, Lt. Col. Blutcher S. Tharp, of Amarillo, along with his fellow officer corps, went through the initiation along with the enlisted men. Tharp wore a neatly trimmed mustache that always appeared to be as much of his uniform as his shirt and trousers. He was placed in the "barber's chair" and one of the sailors promptly whacked half his mustache off. Later Tharp cut the remaining half away, and noted that it was the first time in nearly thirty years that he had been without his beloved mustache.

In the midst of our initiation, a loud whistle blasted over the public address system, followed by the voice of the *Republic* captain: "Now hear this, all hands, a message from the President of the United States: 'This is to let you know that a state of war now exists between the United States and Japan. Govern your actions accordingly. Good luck!'" Within minutes word spread throughout the ship that the Japanese had bombed Pearl Harbor.

War! We were at war with Japan? There was a stunned silence. Everything seemed held in suspended animation. The only sound was the gentle splash of water as our vessel slowly plowed through the sea. We looked nervously at one another as if seeking the answer to a question that had no answer.

The public address system clicked alive after what seemed to be a long, dead silence and the navy crew was instructed to quickly wind up the initiation ceremonies and report to duty stations. Hurriedly, the crew brought its Neptune Rex exercises to a climax, squirting a final few streams of saltwater on some of us and then clearing the decks of the ceremonial gear. The ritual's fervor was gone; a new feeling of urgency permeated the crew and their cargo of mostly young citizen-soldiers, all evidently steaming to war.

The *Republic* and its three sister troop and cargo vessels widened the space between them and launched into a wartime zigzag course. The *Pensacola* poured on the steam and took up a guardian point ahead of the convoy. Occasionally, she would dash around or through the convoy, as if looking for an unseen enemy that might have designs on one or more of our floating hotels. About once daily, the *Pensacola* would disappear over the horizon, and remain out of sight for two or three hours. She constantly launched the tiny, slow-moving scout planes she carried, and the air crews would spend hours circling the region looking for enemy ships.

As we zigzagged west, Japan had launched a massive invasion of the Philippines, our original destination. As a result, our convoy was given a new mission: we were to head south toward Australia until the situation became clearer. We immediately went on wartime alert. Everybody was assigned a duty station on the *Republic*. Our split-trailed French 75mm artillery pieces were brought up from storage in the holds and lashed to the side railings of the ship. Gun crews were assigned to around-the-clock duty on them.

Most of us who were not members of a gun crew were either put on kitchen duty in the bottom hold of the ship, or assigned sky watch on the sun deck. I spent as much time as possible on the latter, since my affinity for kitchen duty was anything but overwhelming.

The southern Pacific remained customarily peaceful during these days of mid-December, as we zigzagged across it at the leisurely pace of eight knots an hour — about the top speed of one of the old buckets in our flotilla. One could become almost mesmerized throbbing along through the South Pacific, across water as flat as the West Texas prairie.

Flying fish constantly sailed beside our ship as if to entertain us. Occasionally we would spot a herd of whales, and on other occasions a big school of jellyfish would bobble alongside our ship as if seeking companionship. Fortunately for us, we were by this time too far south for the Japanese to take notice of us. They were busy with other chores such as recovering the fleet that had attacked Pearl Harbor, and massing for the invasions of the Philippines and Indochina.

The only interruption in our idyllic South Pacific interlude came in mid-December when we pulled into the Fiji Islands to refuel and pick up supplies. The bulk of us stayed aboard the ships while some of our top-ranking officers went ashore to handle the supply details and confer with authorities on whatever mysteries needed discussing. The most exciting incident for most of us was the arrival of a band from the fierce-looking Fijian constabulary, which serenaded us from the dock. Our officers returned with orders to proceed south to Brisbane, Australia, and we headed back to sea. We arrived down under two days before Christmas.

We docked in Brisbane and went ashore, becoming the first American soldiers to have been dispatched from the States and land in a foreign country in World War II. Incidentally, we were told the 131st was among the very first American fighting units to cross the equator. We marched into Brisbane proper after unloading our equipment, and were housed in tents put up at the Ascot Race Track. We were the very first American troops to arrive in Australia, and since nobody had been ahead of us to plan our arrival, we were put on Australian army rations, consisting mostly of mutton and rice.

With our cowboy and cattle heritage, we Texans had little tolerance for sheep herders and no experience with mutton. We gagged on the stuff until we could rummage up some decent food; with what little money we had, we bought some of the scarce beef available on the market. But with the friendliness and hospitality of the Australian people, we could not bring ourselves to complain. The girls were especially nice — most of their men were away fighting with the British against Rommel in North Africa, or trying to slow the southward drive of the Japanese in Malaya and Singapore.

We celebrated Christmas Day 1941 — for most of us, our first Christmas away from home — at the Ascott Race Track in Brisbane. Mutton was the main course, but few of us could stomach the idea — let alone the act — of eating sheep. We refused to consider mutton, a disgusting mass of greasy goo, fit for consumption — not even by our dogs back home. Mercifully, we managed to come up with some rice pudding and a few other favors to make the event more palatable. First Sergeant Wisdom had located Dub Reed and me by this time, and we had the privilege of doing KP duty on Christmas Day.

Our KP duty did not last forever, and we had a few short days following Christmas to enjoy the wonderful Australian hospitality. A liberal leave policy was instituted, and we roamed Brisbane from one end to the other. The Aussies were the first to call us "Yanks." Most of us having descended from members of the Confederate army, we bristled until we learned that "Yank" was the term most English-speaking people used for Americans whether born north or south of the Mason-Dixon line.

"Hi, Yank! Good to have you in Australia. Good on ye, mate!" was a typical greeting as we strolled along the downtown streets of Brisbane.

A few days after our arrival in Australia, on January 2, 1942, Manila fell to the Japanese. The American defenders in the Philippines retreated to Corregidor, where they managed to hold out for more than three months before running out of ammunition.

Meantime, our "holiday" in Brisbane soon came to an end. Just before New Year's Day, 1942, our battalion packed its gear and boarded the SS *Bloemfontein,* a Dutch icebreaker with an impressively curved bow, tied up at one of the Brisbane docks. Word spread that we had been ordered to the Netherlands East Indies island of Java. Until then Java had meant little more than a cup of coffee to most of us. There was a lot of scrambling to find maps with which to locate the place.

There appeared to be some confusion at first over when or if we were to leave the Brisbane harbor. It was just as well that we were delayed for several hours – just before we pulled anchor, Dub Reed came panting up the gangplank from a last-minute excursion in Brisbane.

"I just had to tell that girl goodbye," he explained to our section sergeant, who had been frantically searching for him. "She never would have forgiven me if I hadn't said goodbye!"

The *Bloemfontein* was a fast, modern vessel, and we sped northward up the Australian east coast and along the Great Barrier Reef. Our small convoy rounded the northeastern tip of Australia and anchored in the bay at Port Darwin, Australia's northernmost township. We spent the night there aboard the *Bloemfontein*, nervously watching the sky in the wake of the rumor that Darwin had recently been bombed by the Japanese. The Dutch captain reportedly refused to allow us to unload at Darwin on orders of his government. The following day we headed north again, and nosed into the Timor Sea and Japanese submarine-infested waters.

Our officers received reports that Japanese submarines were very active in this region, as we maneuvered around and between the islands of Sumbawa, Bali, and Java. A torpedo was reportedly sighted, heading toward our ship, but the *Bloemfontein* was a dandy little vessel, and its cruising speed of eighteen knots proved to be our best defense. We again lashed our 75mm guns to the rails around the ship just in case. However, as on the *Republic,* we never had to fire them – fortunately, as it is doubtful that the lashing would have held under their heavy recoil. One report indicated that enemy submarines did in fact sink a ship steaming about two hours behind us.

On January 11, we rounded the eastern tip of Java. Soon a Dutch harbor boat guided us to a pier in Surabaya, Java's major port on its northern coast. It was a somber landing for us, with evidence of recent heavy bombing all around. Ships lay at crazy angles around the harbor, partially sunk and damaged from bombs. Maneuvering through mine fields placed around the harbor by the Dutch, we could see that the docks were a mess.

Our pilot gingerly brought our vessel to one of the piers, and just as the *Bloemfontein* settled in her berth, a nearby air raid alarm sounded. We scurried for cover and waited breathlessly for the incoming bombers. About half an hour later the all clear sounded, indicating the bombers were busy elsewhere. We cautiously moved back onto the dock and began unloading our equipment and personal gear. Dozens of native Javanese squatted on their heels on the docks and passively watched us as we struggled, sweat-soaked, to get our gear and equipment off the *Bloemfontein.* They made not a move to help. We nervously watched the skies and realized for the first time that we had arrived at World War II. Our lives would be permanently changed in less than two months with the Japanese invasion of Java.

4.

Defense of Java

JAVA IS THE MAIN island in what is now Indonesia, a nation that includes Sumatra, south and east Borneo, the Celebes, Bali, and numerous smaller islands. Indeed, Indonesia is the world's largest island group. Indonesia's population has soared to well over one hundred million, with nearly two-thirds living on Java — a slender piece of land about five hundred miles long but less than one hundred miles at its widest section. It has been a republic since 1949, but when we arrived in this lush, equatorial region, it was known as the Netherlands East Indies and had been under Dutch rule for nearly two hundred years.

The native Javanese speak an Austronesian language, although their Dutch landlords and the educated Javanese usually spoke fluent English. Birds and other tropical wildlife flourish, and we soon learned that the Javanese monkey population surpassed its human counterpart. The variety of colorful birds left us speechless. One of the most common was the Java sparrow, a weaverbird that is glaucous gray and black on top with various hues of pink underneath. It has white cheeks and a large pink bill.

As we made our way inland, amazed at every turn, war plans were being formulated elsewhere by the British High Command to counter the new Japanese threat. Nippon had launched a massive southward movement toward Australia, simultaneously with its bombing of Pearl Harbor.

Japanese Lt. Gen. Tomoyuki Yamashita, commanding a force of 125,000 men, 7,320 vehicles, and 11,516 horses, landed at Kota Bharu on the east coast of Malaya on December 8, 1941. This force immediately thrust southward both on land and by sea, placing the British stronghold of Singapore under imminent threat.

The Japanese forces slowly advanced, using pincer movements to surround and eliminate pockets of British resistance. In London, Prime Minister Winston Churchill grew alarmed at the prospect of the loss of the fortress Singapore, and on January 19 issued the following orders to his sizeable force there:

> The entire male population should be employed upon constructing defense works [in Singapore]. The most rigorous compulsion is to be used, up to the limit where picks and shovels are available.
>
> Not only must the defense of Singapore Island be maintained by every means, but the whole island must be fought for until every single unit and every single strong point has been separately destroyed.
>
> Finally, the city of Singapore must be converted into a citadel and defended to the death. No surrender can be accomplished.

The following day, Churchill cabled his Far East commander, Field Marshal the Right Honorable Earl Wavell: "I want to make it absolutely clear that I expect every inch of ground to be defended, every scrap of material or defenses to be blown to pieces to prevent capture by the enemy, and no question of surrender to be entertained until after protracted fighting among the ruins of Singapore City."

While the battle for Singapore raged, a separate battle plan was in the making to defend the Netherlands East Indies, and its mineral-rich islands of Sumatra, Java, Bali, and Timor. Originally, it had been decided to place the I Australian Corps, consisting of some 40,000 troops, on Java for a major defense against the Japanese. Allied forces already on Java, which included the 538 Americans of the 2d Battalion, 131st Field Artillery Regiment, who had landed there January 11, were woefully inadequate for any serious resistance. The major force on Java consisted of a 25,000-man Dutch army that had very little artillery and was unprepared for major fighting. Most of this force, consisting of native Javanese, deserted after the Japanese landed on Java on March 1.

Meanwhile, the Japanese advanced rapidly on every front, threatening northern Burma and India, and Australia itself. General Wavell revised his plans and decided to split the I Australian Corps, sending one division to defend the Australian mainland and the other to counter the growing hostilities along the India-Burma border. Nevertheless, Allied forces countering the enemy throughout Southeast Asia were simply inadequate; Java and the remainder of the Netherlands East Indies were left virtually defenseless before the massive Japanese army converging on the area.

After our battalion unloaded from the *Bloemfontein*, we proceeded inland some thirty-five miles to the Dutch military post, Camp Singasari, near the beautiful little mountain town of Malang. As our motorcade moved to our new post, we noticed that the countryside was thickly populated by the strange, short brown people called Javanese. Children were everywhere. They gathered along the roadside, waving and yelling at us as our caravan passed. It was hard to miss the smiling women. Our medical staff, however, had lectured us before arriving in this incredible land that ninety-seven percent of the "available" women suffered from venereal diseases, warning us to stay away from them. That was all the warning that most of us required.

Camp Singasari was situated on a flat plain between two high mountains. It was made up of modern and clean facilities, and we settled in for what turned out to be a stay of less than two months. An airfield lay about a mile to the south of the camp, and soon after we arrived what remained of the American 19th Bomb Group out of Clark Field, in the Philippines, flew in to continue bombing runs against the expanding Japanese presence. The 19th Bomb Group had barely escaped the Philippines with only their B-17 bombers and very few crewmen. In the next few weeks, mechanics and others from our battalion helped patch up and keep the bombers flying on their missions.

A request came from the bomb group for someone who could type, and since I had studied typing in high school, I volunteered to take a job with the group's adjutant. One day I was invited to take a flight in one of the patched up B-17s, repaired from damage suffered in a recent raid. The flight was scheduled for early the next morning, February 3, and I eagerly looked forward to being on the big plane when it took off. For some reason I overslept that morning. Upon arrival at the hanger, I learned that the B-17 had already taken off. Another member of our battalion, J. E. Bingham, had taken my place, and I'm sure he was as excited about the flight as I had been since neither of us had ever been up in an airplane.

Less than an hour into the flight, a squadron of Japanese Zero fighters swarmed the B-17. The crew was only up for a test flight, and had no ammunition for the machine guns. The Zeros made one pass and shot down the bomber, killing all aboard, including Bingham, my substitute.

This was our very first war casualty. It had a sobering effect on the entire battalion. My own heart pounded relentlessly, and for the very first time the full impact of what we were facing hit me. Bingham was dead; he had been deliberately killed by Japanese soldiers who would do the same thing to the rest of us if and when the opportunity arose.

The Japanese landed on Borneo on January 11 and the Celebes on January 24, capturing both of these islands, which lie just to the north of Java, by February 10. Other Nippon forces landed on Sumatra on February 14, Bali on February 18 and Timor on February 20, leaving the main island of Java surrounded.

Enemy fighters and bombers began showing up regularly over Java in February. We were initiated into the terrifying world of bombardment when twenty-seven Japanese twin-engine bombers appeared over Surabaya and headed straight for Camp Singasari. We barely had time to dive into slit trenches before bombs were falling around us. We lay there helpless, watching petrified as what appeared to be toy airplanes dumped bombs in our direction. Fortunately, their aim was poor, and most of the explosives missed the camp. As the bombers flew out of sight, we cautiously crawled from our trenches and were relieved to find not a single casualty among us.

Since we were in an advanced war zone, it was essential to keep a close eye on our weapons and other supplies, so in due time most of us found ourselves assigned to guard duty around our compound. My turn came on a night of impenetrable darkness. I never was comfortable in the dark, and here I was, as it seemed, a million miles away from home, in a strange land, and alone outside the compound fence while my comrades slept safely inside. I was scared almost to the point of shaking in my army boots.

About an hour into my watch, which had begun at midnight, I noticed flashing lights in the nearby mountains. I concluded that they definitely were signals from a very unfriendly source. My suspicions were confirmed later when we learned that the Japanese had infiltrated the island to set up sophisticated spy networks. It made sense — we had heard enemy broadcasts about American forces landing on Java shortly after our arrival.

For most of us, this was our first experience in the tropics. During guard duty on moonless nights, one's imagination kept the adrenalin racing. The darkness was total. I recalled how my brother, James Thompson, when we were youngsters growing up in Montague County, Texas, described such nights as "dark as the inside of a black cow."

Now that the British, with the only substantial allied military presence in Southeast Asia, had decided not to defend Java, the presence there of our 538 American artillery troops was useful only for propaganda purposes. It was therefore essential that we try to convince the enemy that a large U.S. force was on the island. When we traveled, there was no attempt to disguise our military vehicles and 75mm field guns. We were actually somewhat better armed now than when we had left home. In Hawaii, we had picked up several new British 75s, plus 10,000 rounds of high explosive shells. Prior to this addition, we only had 300 rounds of World War I shrapnel shells, hardly enough to be effective in a serious war. We often drove in convoy in broad daylight, making it easy for enemy reconnaissance planes, which hovered over the area daily, to get good photographs. This tactic must have worked, since the Japanese questioned us extensively after our capture about the location of additional American forces.

The few weeks between our arrival in Java and the landing of the enemy left us with little leisure time, although once or twice we got a few hours off to enjoy the local scenery. One evening about fifty of us broke out our best uniforms, boarded military buses, and headed into the nearby village of Malang. We spent the evening drinking beer and carousing around in those funny little Dutch three-wheeled taxis. Toward midnight, someone produced a bottle of Jack Daniels, and passed it around. Soon it was time to return to Camp Singasari, and in a dizzy swirl we loaded the buses and headed out of town.

It was my misfortune to be one of the last to enter the bus, so I had to move to the back where the only empty seat was beside Lt. Oscar W. Keithly, the Headquarters Battery second-in-command. The bus was filled with mostly drunk soldiers and the tropical night was hot and humid. A few miles out of town the beer and bourbon inside me decided to seek fresh air, and my vomit spilled onto Keithly's legs and ran down his shiny high-top boots. This grave error on my part would have lasting consequences.

Back at Camp Singasari, Jimmy Alexander had traded with the natives for a pet monkey that followed him around like a puppy. He named his new comrade Mac Mac, a term used sometime in the past by English-speaking sailors for sexual intercourse. Java is one of the world's most densely populated regions, and the average age of the residents there must be among the lowest in the world. Children abound and everywhere we traveled herds of boys yelled and waved alongside the roads. Often they would yell "Mac Mac," and there were numerous reports of their bargaining with soldiers for sex with their sisters. Earlier warnings of venereal disease remained sufficient to keep most of us at a distance, however.

It wasn't long before Jimmy had shared his fondness for booze with Mac Mac, and it became a common sight to see Jimmy and his little companion spending their evenings together in a high-spirited fashion. A tipsy monkey is a sight to behold and the two of them seemed to delight in entertaining us with hilarious acts of "monkey business" punctuated with a continuous delivery of Jimmy's witty and intelligent dialogue.

Jimmy was one of those rare characters who seemed to naturally float in and out of trouble. With a little booze under his belt, he would regale his audience with tales of his youth, often citing the fact that his well-to-do father patiently continued financing his education "even after I was kicked out of a dozen colleges."

Being several years senior to most of us teenage privates, Jimmy held us captive during his witty poetic citations. He looked distinguished, with his expertly manicured mustache that perched precisely below a slender nose and friendly, blue eyes.

While Camp Singasari was the scene of our initiation into the horrors of war, it was also a place where humor occasionally broke the seriousness of a bad situation.

As the Japanese bombing and strafing raids began, we quickly learned that our flimsy camp buildings made poor shelters. One day, as the air raid alarm wailed, we hit the trail leading out of camp and into some nearby woods. Lawrence Brown, of Decatur, Texas, a member of Headquarters Battery, led the exodus. He suddenly came upon a small but deep ditch and jumped in feet first. He sank to his waist in a thick, brown sludge, yelling in horror for help. The ditch was an abandoned native toilet.

On another occasion we had just sat down in the dining hall to a meal of fried chicken when the air raid alarm sounded. By this time, we each had designated locations outside the camp area, and when the alarm went off, we began diving out windows and doors, heading for our places. Our section leader, Sergeant Stanbrough, grabbed a handful of chicken and took it with him to the woods.

After our group settled down in our "protected" area, one of our crew, Wilburn W. Rockett, looked longingly at Stanbrough's chicken and decided to go back for some of his own. He had just loaded his arms with food and was headed back to our outpost when a bomb exploded nearby. Rockett's chicken seemed to do some exploding of its own as he hurled it in the air and dived into a shallow trench. He remained foodless until after the raid ended.

Japanese bombing raids on Singasari usually occurred at approximately 10:00 A.M. and 2:00 P.M. — we called them the morning and afternoon runs. At about this time a battery of English Bofers antiaircraft guns arrived in the area. The British gunners were stringing communication lines when one of the afternoon raids hit.

The gunners began lobbing 40mm shells into the air. Suddenly one of the gunners yelled, "I'm hit!" The crew continued stringing communications wire as if nothing was happening. The man who was hit suffered only a minor cut on his arm. The worst casualty among the British gunners was one crewman who dived into a nearby ditch, breaking his false teeth.

The Japanese bombers soon departed, and the British, whose progress had been barely interrupted by the raid, continued with their business of setting up the guns. But at 4:00 P.M. sharp, all work halted, and they began brewing hot tea. It was our first experience with our "tea-sipper" Allies.

After we had been at Camp Singasari for about two weeks, we were ordered to dress in our best uniforms and assemble on the parade ground. We were to be inspected by none other than General Wavell himself. After the inspection, one of our group was overheard saying, "He took one look at us and said, 'My God, all is lost.' "

Later, our supply officer took a truck and driver and went into Malang to buy supplies for the battalion. He returned with the news that the Dutch were appalled over the fact that he was purchasing toilet paper for the enlisted men. "Our enlisted men use a bottle of water and the left hand for that purpose," one Dutch officer informed him.

About three weeks after our arrival in Java, it became obvious that our situation was becoming bleak. As the Japanese drew ever closer, the remnants of the 19th Bomb Group prepared to evacuate to Australia. There was a report that the Air Corps offered to take the 131st with them, but we were under direct command of the Dutch government on Java and were ordered to stay and help defend the island against the impending invasion.

When the Second World War ended, General Douglas MacArthur, the supreme allied commander in Japan, ordered the Japanese government to prepare monographs detailing various war operations. Monograph Number 66 deals with plans for the invasion of Java. It was prepared by Col. Akimitsu Oda, a former staff officer of the Japanese 16th Army, commanded by Lt. Gen. Hitoshi Imamura.

Oda's work provides evidence that Japan was making war plans well in advance of the attack on Pearl Harbor. As early as November 19, 1941, General Imamura and his staff had completed details for the invasion and capture of the mineral-rich Netherlands East Indies, with emphasis placed on Java.

Simultaneously with the attack on Pearl Harbor, Japanese forces launched a leapfrog operation south toward Australia. One of the first pieces of territory secured was Jolo, a small island west of Mindanao in the Philippines chain. There they began assembling troops for the invasion of Java. Other forces were being concentrated at Cam Ranh Bay on the east coast of French Indochina. On January 14, 1942, the Japanese 48th Division was placed under the command of the 16th Army and sent to Jolo. At the same time, the 2d Division and several other units made ready for the invasion at Cam Ranh Bay.

Japanese intelligence estimated Allied strength in the Netherlands East Indies to be about 85,000 men, "with a large proportion of this force being natives who were considered very poor fighters." According to Australian historian Lionel Wigmore, in his book *The Japanese Thrust,* the Allies, in addition to a scattering of naval warships in the area, had in their air forces on Java some eighteen British fighter planes and twenty twin-engine aircraft fit for operations, a few American fighters (mostly P-40s), and ten heavily depleted Dutch squadrons. Ground forces consisted of the Dutch army of 25,000 (mostly native Javanese considered incapable of effective resistance), two Australian battalions (2/3 Machine Gun and 2/2 Pioneers) under the command of Brigadier A. S. Blackburn; a squadron of British tanks of the 3d Hussars; and the 2d Battalion, 131st Field Artillery, the only U.S. contingent on the island.

General Imamura was finalizing his invasion plans on Formosa and received orders on January 20 to launch the invasion of Java. He coordinated his land forces' plans with commanders of the Japanese 3d Air Group, 3d Fleet, and 11th Air Fleet. The air fleet was to consist of 180 army and 240 navy planes. Troop assembly for the invasion took longer than planned.

Finally, on February 18, the first Japanese convoy of fifty-six ships left its anchorage at Cam Ranh Bay, escorted by the 5th Destroyer Squadron. At noon on February 22, the Japanese navy requested postponement of the attack on Java for two days due to reports of an Allied fleet of three large cruisers, five medium cruisers and eight destroyers operating in the Java Sea. The invasion force reversed its course and began to stall. On February 23, it resumed its southward journey toward Java. On February 19, the 48th Division, escorted by the 4th Destroyer Squadron and the 23d Air Fleet, left Jolo headed for the east coast of Java. This force was also delayed, resuming its southward movement on February 25.

Two days later, the invasion fleet escorting the Japanese 48th Division ran into Allied naval forces, and a fierce battle ensued in the Sunda Strait, a fairly shallow passage between Java and Sumatra. The Allied force consisted of the American heavy cruiser USS *Houston* and the Australian light cruiser HMAS *Perth*. The two cruisers had been ordered to escape through Sunda Strait and sail to Australia. They were rounding Bantam Bay, just east of the entrance to Sunda Strait, when they found a line of Japanese transports at anchor. They sunk four of these and damaged several others before the Japanese covering force of three cruisers and nine destroyers arrived. The Japanese battle fleet encircled the *Houston* and the *Perth*, and launched a heavy gun and torpedo attack. Records later indicated that the Japanese destroyed several of their own vessels in the ensuing confusion.

The *Houston* and *Perth* were torpedoed and shelled relentlessly, and after putting up a gallant fight, both were sunk. Each ship lost about 70 percent of its crew in the battle. Many of the survivors were in the oil-slick waters off the Java coast for up to forty-eight hours before reaching land. They later joined us in Japanese prisoner of war camps.

The Allied fleet that included the *Houston* and *Perth* was heavily outnumbered by the Japanese, but the extent of the odds were not known until March 17, when England's Lord Strabolgi said he was compelled to let the world know what happened in the battle of Sunda Strait. He told the British Parliament that the Japanese fleet opposing the *Houston* and *Perth* consisted of fourteen cruisers, five aircraft carriers, fifty-five destroyers and twenty-five submarines.

While these violent events unfolded off the coast of Java, the bulk of our battalion was ordered to move toward the west end of Java and join other scattered Allied units in an effort to check the major Japanese invasion. Dutch Lt. Gen. H. ter Poorten commanded Allied ground forces on Java. British General Wavell and several senior American and Australian officers had departed Java on February 25, obviously convinced the Allies could not defend the territory. All of our units except E Battery loaded up and our little armada pulled out of Camp Singasari late on February 28. Our E Battery was left behind to assist in the defense of Surabaya and the eastern end of Java. The rest of us headed west toward Batavia, the capital city of Java, renamed Jakarta when the Indonesians gained their independence after the war.

Shortly after returning home, while convalescing in Madigan General Hospital at Fort Lewis, Washington, I recorded in a stenographer's notebook some of my memories of our little war against the Japanese in March 1942. I still have that notebook and feel the account is worthy of inclusion here, although with the passage of some fifty years, some of the details of those events sound strange:

> During the night of February 28, Nippon landed troops at four places on Java. We were routed out early the following morning and headed for the opposite (west) end of the island to give artillery support to the few Australian pioneers (infantry/engineers) trying to slow the largest landing force headed toward Batavia.
>
> Upon leaving Soerabaja [Surabaya], the main port on the eastern end of Java, someone got the bright idea that while our motorcade journeyed across the country we would do so during daylight hours in order to boost the morale of the Dutch. Here we were, all 400 of us, boldly dashing across the backbone highway of Java in broad daylight, throwing caution to the winds. Rumor had it that the Japs outnumbered us 240 to 1 in troops, and 179 to 0 in airplanes, although this

number of aircraft later would be doubled several times. We would pass through a village, make a wide sweep, rearrange our vehicles and enter that village from another direction. It all seemed useless to me, but then the idea was to make the people think they had tons of support from the United States Army, which, according to the Dutch, had been promised them after America became involved in the war.

We spent three days madly dashing around all over the place, finally winding up near the town of Buitenzorg, about sixty miles from the west end of Java. Lucky for us enemy aircraft never once attacked while we were dashing around in broad daylight. Meanwhile, the Japanese had made all their landings on Java with little initial opposition. This must have puzzled them since our propaganda appeared to have convinced them there was a sizable American fighting force on the island.

We set up forward headquarters in a rubber plantation about two and a half miles back of the Australian front line. A detail was sent to contact the Australians, who had checked the Japanese advance temporarily along the banks of a small river. The Dutch had blown up a bridge across the river. The Japanese had an estimated 40,000 troops on their side of the stream, and we had 2,500 Australian infantry supported by our one dozen 75 millimeter artillery pieces. When we arrived at the front lines we were issued old Army Springfield rifles minus bayonets, a gun most of us had never seen before, let alone fired. Our arms also consisted of several .50-caliber machine guns attached to Jeeps. The Australians had rifles, with bayonets, a few Tommy guns and some mortars. Opposing us was a formidable enemy armed with modern rifles and sharp, shiny bayonets, light and heavy machine guns, light and heavy artillery, tanks, and supported by plenty of aircraft. And don't forget those effective 2.4 [inch] mortars that inflict so much damage.

Our artillery went into action on the morning of March 4 a few hundred yards back of the Australian lines, firing on Japanese positions until dark. Forward observers reported direct hits on several troop concentrations, four medium tanks destroyed, and about ten mortars silenced. The Japanese seemed to become very upset at having 75mm shells ripping into their positions. They sent out small patrols in an effort to locate and destroy these guns, but were unsuccessful.

During the next couple of days our artillery changed positions several times and continued pelting the Japanese. At one point I asked Major Rogers how things were going at the front.

"There's only a few hundred of them over there," he replied optimistically. "We'll have them wiped out by tomorrow noon, and within a week there won't be a Jap left on Java."

I was very fond of the major, my first commanding officer when I first joined the National Guard a couple of years earlier, but he must have known what the real situation was on the front. He always was saying something to boost morale, and usually we accepted his statements without question. It really helps to convince one that everything is okay, even if it isn't.

One amusing interlude involving everybody's friend Jimmy Alexander occurred during our three-day battle. Jimmy always managed to have what appeared to be an endless supply of booze and shortly after the firing at the front heated up, Jimmy, who was feeling no pain at the time, decided to go up there and see for himself who was winning the war. He climbed atop a truck loaded with ammunition and off they went to the front. About an hour later, the same truck came back to the bivouac area without its ammunition, but containing a white-faced Jimmy who definitely was somewhat more sober than when he had left our camp.

"Boy," he said. "It sure doesn't take much of that to get a belly full!"

But before the day was over, he had a few more belts and built up enough courage to go back to where the fighting was raging. His same pasty-faced reappearance came in short order, but finally he had convinced himself that his place really was back with the rest of us in our forward position, hiding under the trees in the rubber plantation.

Later, recalling the few days while the battle raged in Java, Dan C. Buzzo of Headquarters Battery remembered spending a lot of time in a trench holding his hands to his ears.

"You get scared to death," Buzzo recalled. "The Aussies would say, 'Come on, Yank, you wanna give them a little cold steel?' I'd say, 'No, thanks, I think I'll stay here.' "

During the evening of March 5, while we still were delaying the Japanese advance northwest of Buitenzorg, Stanbrough and Sgt. I. O. "Little" Offerle of D Battery posted some guards along the route of retreat and decided to look for some food.

They spied a large, modern hotel and parked their command car at the front entry. It turned out to be the Savoy, a luxurious place with a fountain in front and white, deep rugs on the floor. There was a big party going on inside, so the two GIs went in to investigate.

"There were dozens of Dutch officers in dress uniform and their women were elegantly dressed in formal wear," Stanbrough recalled. "They were being served a seven course dinner and a good orchestra was playing. It was a formal ball in progress.

"We entered right off the road, dressed in our fatigues, dirty and bearded, and carrying our .45 pistols. We were utterly amazed to see this big party going on with bright lights blazing with a full-scale war going on just down the road."

The Americans managed to get seated at the elegant dinner party and gorged themselves at what appeared to be the Dutch's last fling, held before the Japanese could move into the area.

Toward the end of the day on March 7, a courier from the front came to our camp with the following message from our commanding officer, Colonel Tharp: "The Australian Brigadier says it's getting pretty hot up there. He advised an immediate withdrawal. The first line of Japs already have crossed the river. We can't possibly stop them — we're outnumbered at least 100 to 1."

Colonel Tharp, who had set up his command post in the nearby town of Buitenzorg [now Bogor], radioed the following message: "All Batteries report here [to Buitenzorg] immediately with equipment. Be prepared to withdraw to new positions by 9:00 P.M. Urgent!"

The impact of this hit us like a ton of bricks. At last we fully realized that the war had caught up with us. As we began pulling out of the rubber plantation, this moonless night appeared to be the darkest since I stood guard in Camp Singasari. The first sergeant had told me to stay until the last vehicle had cleared the rubber plantation, since my command car held the radio equipment that kept us in touch with our command post in Buitenzorg. I was instructed to radio ahead if anything went wrong, as if that would do any good should the Japanese suddenly move in.

All but the last truck had cleared the area, and it was stuck in a low, muddy spot in the grove. We frantically worked to free the truck, knowing the enemy was just over the way and would be upon us in no time. Finally, it was freed, and we sped out of the trees and onto the nearby paved roadway. Retreating! And I thought we practically had them whipped. Faster! Faster! They're right behind you! And incidentally, you're the last car between our own forces and the enemy. I panicked and turned on my headlights, a violation of the blackout that had been imposed. The command car was going faster and faster, and cold chills were running up and down my spine. Speeding past an intersection, I glanced to my right and saw the shadowy outline of military vehicles lined up for some distance. I never knew if they were friend or foe, choosing instead to try and coax some more speed out of my vehicle.

Finally I caught up with the tail end of our convoy, and got my own tail end chewed out for having my headlights shining. After daybreak the next day a Japanese airplane flew over our area at a low altitude, obviously looking for us.

"Get under cover down there — get that damned car out of sight," one of our officers yelled. I scurried under some trees, fearing the Japanese pilot may have heard him yell at me. We camped that night in a heavily wooded spot that turned out to be near an Australian army supply depot. The word spread quickly and a goodly number of us set out to raid the big warehouse. We found it full of cigarettes and army issue rum. We loaded our pockets and arms with all we could carry, and had a big party that night.

It was at this spot that Pvt. B. E. "Dusty" Rhodes was acci-
dentally shot and killed by a friend who was cleaning his rifle.
The next morning the colonel gathered us around him and
said: "Well, men, it's quite obvious that we aren't running the
Japs off the island and we aren't likely to. It looks like this
whole thing will fall through. We are under the direct command of the Dutch, and what they say, we have to do. I think
they will surrender by the tenth at the latest. We have one
chance left. There may be a ship down on the south coast.
We'll try to make it through to it."

Air raid warnings sounded with growing frequency. We
pulled into a large clump of bamboo. That morning we saw
what looked like hundreds of Japanese bombers flying in perfect formation over Batavia. At about 11:00 A.M. on March 8 a
Dutch messenger from Batavia came in on a motorcycle with
the following message: "We are forced to surrender. It is useless to try to hold out any longer. You are ordered to surrender immediately with your men and equipment, unconditionally, to the Imperial Japanese Army. You are to wait with your
men and equipment at Goerett [a nearby town]."

"Whose orders are these?" Colonel Tharp asked.

"The Governor General's office, Batavia, sir," was the re-
ply. "I also am instructed to tell you that it's useless to attempt
an escape. There is no way out." The Dutch officer's tone was
final. The Dutch government on Java had capitulated, given
up, quit, surrendered.

We all were stunned, speechless. Some of us were crying
out of fear of an uncertain future. A few of our men slipped
out of camp against orders and headed for the nearby coast
in hopes that there would be one chance in a thousand for
some means of escape. But there was none; within days they
would be rounded up and impounded with the others. Although it took some time to penetrate our bewildered minds,
we must have known it from the moment the Dutch officer
had given us orders to surrender. We were prisoners of war,
at the mercy of strange, foreign forces which had been doing
their best to kill us these past few weeks. A great, black cloud
of hopelessness seemed to envelop us. We had lost control of
our own destiny.

5.

The Surrender

HOW DOES ONE prepare to submit to an enemy as unknown, as strange, as if he were from another planet? Nobody offered any advice — nobody had any to offer, so as the initial shock brought by word of surrender passed, some of us went about doing what we could to lessen the impact of defeat. Gun crews removed and destroyed the firing pins of our big artillery pieces. I took my trusty old .45-caliber pistol from its holster and slung it into a nearby lake. I had carried that sidearm through the Louisiana Maneuvers, on countless field exercises, across the western United States, over the Pacific Ocean, in Australia, and then into battle in Java. I was not about to give it up to some Jap soldier who might fire it back at me.

Late on the afternoon of March 8, we assembled on a roadside near the town of Goerett, unloaded, and waited there in silent agony. Soon all of our vehicles were taken away and we were left on foot with only our personal gear. We camped out in tents, and unsurprisingly, there was little sleep that first night in captivity. Sometime during the night it rained. A cold fear gripped me as I tried to sleep. The fear tied my stomach in knots and there was a dull ache that started at the base of my tongue and drilled deep into my bowels. There was little or no conversation among us that night, and when one spoke, it was in a low, hushed tone that reflected our anxious uncertainty.

The next morning we crawled out of our makeshift beds into damp, cool air — and the full realization that we were prisoners of war, that it had not been just a nightmare.

As if giving our appalling situation form, the ground all around our compound was littered with huge, black scorpions. They looked hideous — swollen, hairy insects crawling into our living nightmare straight from a Hollywood horror movie — but turned out to be less threatening than disgusting as they were sluggish and exhibited little aggression. Nonetheless, we avoided any contact with them. Within a couple of hours they had crawled into nearby brush and disappeared. We gave them no further thought; more weighty matters confronted us.

The next day we marched to a suburb of Goerett, and were housed in a large two-story warehouse. We spent a week there, never once coming into direct contact with our conqueror, although a delegation of our officers had been driven into town to meet with the Japanese. During one of those nights several of us were aroused from sleep by two Javanese women who were crawling among us, apparently looking for loot. The older woman — apparently the mother of the younger one — began stammering, "Mac Mac," perhaps trying to convince us she was only there for some loving. Both women were escorted out of the building and told in sign language that they might have their throats cut if they returned.

We spent a restless week in that Goerett warehouse, mostly staring into space and cultivating ulcers. Then we were ordered to line up outside on the street with all our gear and were marched to the Goerett railway station where we had our first physical encounter with the Japanese. Heavily armed guards were standing in formation when we arrived, and they quickly surrounded us, yelling and screaming in a language that most of us had never before encountered.

This was our first close-up look at the enemy. These fierce little men were so strange and threatening that our first reaction was, "they're just going to kill us and get it over with." Typically, the Japanese soldier stood about five feet, six inches tall. He wore a comical little head piece much like the hats we now describe as "gimmie caps." His loose-fitting, short-sleeved shirt was stuffed inside baggy trousers that seemed to be two sizes too large. Many soldiers wore horn-rimmed glasses, and not a few flashed some gold teeth when they were yelling at us. The strangest part of their military uniform were the odd black tennis shoes that were slit at the front, separating the big toe from the other four toes.

They wielded their rifle butts and threatened us with bayonets, screeching *"Speedo, Speedo,"* in high-pitched voices, jumping around like monkeys, getting us to hustle onto the train boxcars. I was scared speechless, and it was this first personal encounter with the Japs that led me to form a mental pact with myself. I vowed to try to remain as inconspicuous as possible. Any time there was a group of POWs, I would always try to position myself in the middle or toward the back of the formation. This proved to be a handy plan for survival, although at six feet, two inches tall, it was hard at times for me to remain inconspicuous.

Our first prison camp was a group of filthy, lice-infested barracks that formerly housed Javanese soldiers of the Dutch army, conscripted laborers for Malay rice fields, and some disciplinary work groups. It was located in the coastal town of Tanjong Priok, which served as the port facility of the capital city of Batavia. We spent about five weeks there before moving into the heart of Batavia, where we were housed at a former Dutch army post called Bicycle Camp. It was here that we first ran into survivors of the USS *Houston,* the heavy cruiser sunk early on March 1 in the battle of Sunda Strait. Bicycle Camp also housed Australian, British, and Dutch prisoners, about three thousand POWs altogether.

Many of the sailors and Marines who survived the sinking of the *Houston* barely managed to get ashore, escaping death with only the oil-soaked clothes on their back. We were delighted to run into fellow Americans and gladly shared our few personal effects with them.

We soon settled into a routine at Bicycle Camp, although we had to be on our toes when a Jap guard came into our quarters. Two Japanese sergeants at Bicycle actually ran the camp. One was a Korean, who claimed to be a Christian and treated us with some kindness. The other turned out to be a typical Japanese soldier insofar as his relationship with lowly POWs went. We called him the Brown Bomber because of his habit of bashing a prisoner in the face or gut with his rifle butt for the sheer pleasure of it.

The Japanese Imperial Army practiced severe discipline even among themselves. They liberally used corporal punishment in their own ranks, and naturally applied their methods to us after we became their captives. The most common form of punishment was to be slapped in the face, or belted on the chin with a fist. Next in frequency was the use of anything available as a weapon. Often it was the rifle butt, or the point of a rifle. At other times, it was bamboo poles of various sizes. Frequently, punishment lost all sense of restraint or proportion; later, in the Burma jungles, there would be several instances where prisoners were beaten to death as punishment for minor infractions.

As soon as we had settled into the barracks at Bicycle Camp, the Japanese began taking groups of fifty to one hundred POWs outside on work parties, mostly to the docks to load and unload ships. Some work parties went to the Batavia airport to repair bombed runways and buildings. Prisoners were lined up in formation and marched out the only gate at Bicycle Camp and herded through the downtown streets to their work sites. The Japanese delighted in marching us through heavily populated areas to show the natives that the little brown men were masters of the big white men.

Without question, the native Javanese had welcomed the Japanese conquerors as liberators, as they had been under the colonial rule of the Dutch since 1632. When the Japanese invaded Java, most of the Javanese, who made up the bulk of the Dutch army, deserted. As the conquering forces marched in, the Javanese turned out by the millions to greet them, waving and smiling. Thousands of little Japanese flags, which they called the Rising Sun, appeared in the hands of the natives. The Japanese had been flooding the airwaves with propaganda phrases touting "Asia for the Asiatics." The Japanese also wooed native populations throughout Southeast Asia with a program they called the Greater Southeast Asia Co-prosperity Sphere. Under this scheme, they claimed to have plans for "sharing" the wealth of the region with native populations after they jointly threw the white man out.

The Javanese, like natives of other countries enveloped by the Japanese expansion, doubtlessly thought their new "partners" would be a vast improvement over the European colonial governments that had been ruling them. It didn't take long, however, for them to realize that the Japanese were interested in material gain only, having little or no regard for the welfare of the natives. As soon as they had consolidated their control of Java, the Japanese began systematically looting the island of everything they could get their hands on. Often as we marched through the streets of Batavia, we saw Japanese soldiers beating both male and female civilians. In a matter of a few months, the Javanese longed for a return of the Dutch — a fate better by far than the savage occupation by Nippon.

As we established a semblance of routine at Bicycle Camp, an unpleasant incident occurred among the Americans, an incident many to this day prefer not to acknowledge. The affair created much anguish, but it happened, and though the particulars are distasteful, they should be aired.

When we were captured, our officers managed to keep control of a large sum of cash — in American dollars — which had been issued to buy supplies and to meet payrolls for the 2d Battalion. One report listed the total at about $150,000. During those first few months of captivity in Java, the Japanese allowed us to purchase food outside the camp to augment the meager rations of rice and watery stew they allotted us. It didn't take long for most of us — especially the enlisted men who had very little to begin with — to run out of personal funds. But the officers had plenty, and at first spent it only on themselves. While the enlisted men existed on rice and water-stew, the officers dined on pinto beans, meats, fruits, and other delicacies that were easily obtainable through local markets.

Soon there was considerable grumbling among the enlisted men, and some of the noncommissioned officers got together and delegated M.Sgt. E. E. Shaw, our highest ranking NCO, to take the gripes to the officers. Shaw met with some of the officers and apparently threatened to take the issue up after the war. He was hauled up before a court-martial and reduced in rank to private for thirty days. His punishment would have been more severe had not Major Rogers intervened on his behalf. As it turned out, the confrontation had its desired effect. Shortly thereafter, funds were used to buy extra food for all Americans in the camp, and we ate fairly well for the remainder of our stay in Bicycle Camp. (This incident did not surface after the war, primarily because Shaw was among those who did not survive the Death Railway atrocities.)

Later, our officers showed courage on our behalf. In early July the Japanese ordered all prisoners in Bicycle Camp to sign a statement swearing that they would not try to escape. Since the Geneva Convention prohibits forcing POWs to sign such an oath, everyone at first refused. The Japanese were furious, and they began beating our higher ranking officers and threatening to shoot some prisoners.

On July 3, Capt. Arch L. Fitzsimmons, the Headquarters Battery commander, and other commanders, called their noncommissioned officers into conference and told them to have all the men sign the oath. "I'm ordering you to do so on my own responsibilty," Fitzsimmons said.

By July 4 — Independence Day back home — everybody had signed, after some more Japanese persuasion conducted with heavy bamboo clubs. The Japanese were still furious. They cut our rations and halted our outside trips to buy supplementary food. After some weeks, however, their fury abated and things settled down.

The next seven months at Bicycle Camp were, in retrospect, a pleasant interlude when compared with what we were about to go through. Most of us who remained relatively healthy had to go outside camp on work parties regularly, and while the work was often strenuous, it was not the life-threatening ordeal we would be put through later in Burma and Thailand. Often on work parties we were able to make illicit contact with the locals and would trade for or purchase extra rations to supplement the unappetizing rice diet that was our daily fare.

Stanbrough, our radio section chief, was, appropriately, fascinated by radio electronics. Soon after we settled into prison life at Bicycle Camp, he began collecting the necessary parts for a radio. One of these items was copper wire, and some of us always were on the lookout for this and other materials. One day, Stanbrough told Dub Reed that he still needed some copper wire and told him to search for it during a work trip outside the camp. There was a lot of material around the docks where most of us worked, and sure enough, Reed found about one hundred feet of fine copper wire. He carefully wrapped it around his torso under his clothing, and when our work was finished, we began the march back to camp. It was at about this time in our captivity that the Japanese guards began cracking down on us, and as we marched into camp through the big pillars at the main gate, the guards halted everybody and began searching us for booty.

They found the copper wire on Reed, and began beating him savagely. After searching the rest of us, they let all of us except Reed go to our barracks. Reed was kept at the guardhouse, and after some more beatings, was made to squat in front of the guardhouse with a bamboo pole about four inches in diameter lodged behind his knees. Reed was forced to kneel in this position for about twenty-four hours. When he finally was released, he had to be carried to his bunk, and it was several days before he could again walk normally. This type of torture turned out to be a commonplace method employed by our captors.

Meanwhile, the Brown Bomber kept us alert and made life a continuous frenzy of fear and misery. He obviously enjoyed bursting into barracks unannounced and rigorously punishing anyone caught in the slightest infraction. One day, when my name failed to turn up on the outside work party roster, I took advantage of the day off and did some personal housekeeping chores. Then, as the warm tropical climate worked its magic spell, I fell asleep in my bunk. The Brown Bomber happened to pick this moment for one of his unscheduled inspections, and with yells and curses, proceeded through the building belting first one and then another prisoner just for the thrill of it. He was so worked up by the time he got to the middle of the room — where my bunk was — that he failed to see me, lying in deep slumber. The fact that my bunk was the upper of a double helped conceal me, otherwise I likely would have been beaten unconscious.

During the early weeks of our captivity, a General Electric portable radio about the size of a small bread box turned up, and ultimately made its way to Stanbrough, our resident electronics wizard. Stanbrough said the set had been brought into camp by

Sgt. Jack Carney. He then went to work on the radio, repairing considerable damage and rewinding the coils for shortwave reception. Soon he was able to pick up the British Broadcasting Corporation newscasts from London and India. Occasionally we could bring in shortwave broadcasts from San Francisco.

After completing his masterful reclamation, Stanbrough secreted the aerial in an out-of-the-way place in the attic of our barracks. He and Ficklin bunked together and they listened to BBC newscasts on a regular basis. The radio was hidden inside the corner post of their bunk and was powered by electricity from a wire extending out of the ceiling of our building. Around noon one day, Stanbrough was listening to the radio over the repeated protests of Ficklin.

On this occasion, Stanbrough was in his upper bunk listening by earphone to the radio when a Japanese guard suddenly entered our building and strode briskly down the center aisle. Stanbrough could not hear the sudden scream of *"Kioski!"* (Attention!) which we had to yell when a guard entered the barracks. As the guard approached the area where Stanbrough lay in his bunk, the bayonet on his rifle gently scraped against the electrical wire running from the light socket to the radio. The guard marched to the end of the barracks, turned about and came back up the aisle. Again, the bayonet scraped the wire, making it gently sway. But the guard, intent on trying to find somebody to punish, failed to notice Stanbrough or his radio.

Possession of a radio was a most serious offense, with the possessor facing the possibility of execution, or at least a severe bashing. The incident gave strength to Ficklin's argument against frequent use of the radio, and thereafter Stanbrough was more discreet in pursuing his listening habits.

With a good 50 percent of us not included in the daily outside work parties, we wound up with some leisure time on our hands. We turned from talking about when the war would end to reading and playing cards. It was during these first few months of captivity that I learned to play bridge. The Japanese had allowed us to keep most of our personal possessions, and we, like other soldiers before and after, loved to play cards, and there were plenty of decks available. There also were a good number of books; they came in handy during some of the warm, tropical days when we had little to do but lounge on our homemade bunks and keep a leery eye out for the ever-present guard. The game of bridge came easily for me, and I plunged into it enthusiastically.

One of the Australians in Bicycle Camp had been involved in the entertainment business before the war, and he set out to organize some entertainment groups. As a teenager, I had been a member of a quartet in our Baptist church in Wichita Falls. I used this background to join a male chorus of about a dozen British and Australians. A piano graced the camp, and soon our chorus was singing some of the old barbershop harmonies during the evenings to entertain our fellow captives. We got pretty good, and soon our singing group was told that we were to go into town to a radio station and perform with a Dutch orchestra. Our assigned tune was "In the Good Old Summertime." We practiced it over and over until we had it down to perfection. We dressed up in our best uniform — we still had most of our clothing — boarded a truck, and were driven into the heart of Batavia.

The broadcast studio was on a side street, and as we entered it we were greeted in a most friendly manner by a Japanese civilian who spoke excellent California-accented English. He told us to relax and sing our very best, after which he would allow us to voice our names over the air. Following the broadcast, our host told us that he had worked for one of the big studios in Hollywood more than twenty years before the war. He said that he had received a telegram just before hostilities began, informing him that a close relative was desperately ill and that he was to return to Japan immediately. Upon arrival, he was conscripted by the army and put in their propaganda section. We were told the broadcast that day was an English language program beamed to Australia.

While we never learned if the singing or the reading of our names were picked up by the Allies, the trip did serve a good purpose: we were given a delicious meal and a large bottle of the best Dutch beer available. It was a memorable interlude, but did little to prepare us for what was ahead.

Back in Bicycle Camp, our routine primarily consisted of trying to stay out of the sight and reach of the guards, playing some cards, reading a book, or working at the docks. Like soldiers everywhere, most of our talk in those early days of captivity was about girls. Later, when rations reached the starvation level, priorities would shift and our attention would move to conversations about food. One of the games we played then was to see who could come up with the most tantalizing menu.

Gradually, the full impact of what was happening to us hit me. I began to think about the future. Since I had been brought up in a Christian home, I instituted a ritual of regularly praying each night. My father, Kyle Sr., was a country Baptist preacher, and religion had been an important part of our lives. I had professed Christianity and was baptized at fourteen. In retrospect, I believe that God placed His protective arms around me at the time of our capture and kept them there throughout our forty-two-month ordeal that so often was pure hell on earth. Early on I adopted a simple prayer: "Lord, I know I am in a lot of trouble. I believe you can help me, and I want to live through this and go home again if it is Your will. But if it is not Your will, I will accept whatever happens." I prayed a version of this same petition virtually every night for the next three and one-half years, and can say with conviction that it gave me strength when I had none of my own.

When we were not playing cards or reading, we frequently gathered in small groups for the bull sessions that are a common part of a soldier's life. How long the war might last was one of our favorite subjects. In my naivete, I quickly adopted an optimistic attitude: The war will end within three months. Thus, I literally lived the coming years three months at a time. In April, I would tell myself that the Americans would rescue us by July. When July rolled around and no Americans appeared, I would simply extend the end of the war until October — and then all this nonsense would be over. Others were less optimistic.

Noel T. Mason, of Fort Worth, was pessimistic, but more realistic than me. To my prediction of a short war, he replied, "Don't you believe it. This will be a long, drawn-out affair and we're going to see a lot of hell before it is over." He paused, then added, "You and I are going to have to eat a thousand cups of rice before we get home. Maybe even more."

Mason saw, far more clearly than most of us, past our youthful optimism, into the gloom of the coming ordeal. He died in 1967 of cancer, no doubt brought on by the hardships inflicted on our group during the very hell he forsaw.

With the Stanbrough radio in regular operation, we had some idea of the war's progress, and the more optimistic of us firmly believed that our confinement would be short-lived. Jimmy Alexander had a different response to this crucial topic. After the subject had been thoroughly discussed and dissected, Alexander came up with a dandy little poem — one of his specialties — that succinctly reveals this fascinating man's character and wit:

When the War Will End
As recited by James G. Alexander

Of absolute knowledge I have none,
But my aunt's, sister's, husband's son
Heard a policeman on his beat
Say to a pedestrian he happened to meet
That he had a letter just last week
That was written in the finest Greek
From a Chinese coolie in Timbuktu
Who claimed he heard of a fellow who knew
Of a certain guy in a Texas town
Who got it straight from a circus clown
That a group of South American Jews
Had undertaken to prove the news
That a high society female crook
Had written in a special book
That she had a friend and her friend had a friend
That knew just when the war would end.

Even after captivity, without his beloved booze, Jimmy's keen mind would produce jaunty, intelligent prose and verse which did so much to keep our spirits from sinking into the soles of our rotting army boots. Jimmy, like so many of our comrades, did not come home from the depths of the Burmese jungles. But his words did.

As the warm tropical days turned toward what would be autumn back home, wheels turned elsewhere that would change our lives forever. One phase of the Japanese master plan was for its forces to press eastward through Burma and invade India, then a major British colonial empire of 750 million people. The Japanese assembled a large army in western Burma which ran into a formidable force of British troops there that included the Gurkas and Sikhs, the indomitably fierce soldiers who made up a great share of the British colonial armed forces.

The fighting soon bogged down in a stalemate, and the Japanese began having trouble supplying their deadlocked armies. Nippon had established its headquarters in Rangoon, and supplies for these forces, mostly coming from Japan, depended on the long and exposed sea route down through the South China Sea, around Singapore, then up through the Strait of Malacca and the Andaman Sea. This was a long haul for the Japanese merchant fleet, consisting of old, slow ships that would be exposed to growing Allied air and sea forces during the journey. The Japanese sought — and found — a better way.

Before the Second World War, the British had surveyed a 260-mile stretch of jungles from Thanbyuzayat, Burma, southward into Thailand, where the Thai rail system ended at the village of Ban Pong. They had abandoned the survey line, however, because of the difficulties involved, including the numerous tropical diseases endemic to the region. To attempt such a feat, the British had concluded, would be too costly both in human life and in material.

But that was Western philosophy for you, and the Japanese apparently had an entirely different view regarding humanity, especially where it concerned humanity other than their own. Nippon desperately needed an overland route to supply its large army in western Burma, and it naturally turned to the old British survey for the solution. The Japanese too had been handed an unexpected bonus upon their capture of Singapore and the Netherlands East Indies. They suddenly and unexpectedly were the warders of tens of thousands of healthy, young enemy soldiers who sat idle in the teeming prison camps scattered over the region. The labor problem was solved. By the middle of September 1942, the trek toward the infamous "Death Railway" had begun.

Japanese surveyors first studied the British plans and concluded that the railroad would take five years to build, given the thick jungles, heavy rains, numerous rivers, and rugged, rocky terrain. The estimate proved unacceptable to the Imperial Army, which ordered the line completed by November 1943, approximately fifteen months away.

In Texas, the War Department had notified our parents that the battalion was "missing in action and presumed prisoners of war." Parents and other close family members began meeting to gather strength from one another, and by the end of 1942, they began calling themselves families of the "Lost Battalion." In a letter published during that time in the *Fort Worth Star-Telegram,* my mother wrote:

> But wherever K.O. is, he's all right. He won't complain and he can take it. His only worry will be about his mother and father to whom he has been a blessing for 19 years. We can not help but believe that our boy, as well as the other members of the Battalion, will be returned to their families some day.

> Mrs. A. R. Gordon, mother of Sgt. Crayton R. Gordon, of Fort Worth, wrote, "I know many of the boys who are now in Java and particularly do I remember Sergeants Billy Joe Mallard and Wade H. Webb, both of Hillsboro. I was closely associated with these young men of the 'Lost Battalion.' I know the ability of those boys and know that they can meet whatever faces them like men. I am proud of the boys and of their brave parents." In tribute, Mrs. Gordon wrote a poem which concluded:

> > They call them the Lost Battalion,
> > But this can never be;
> > For they will live forever
> > In our nation's history.

As our families rallied, preparations were underway in Java to ship all POWs to other, undisclosed locations. As we prepared to leave, the Japanese gave each of us an international post card and said that we could address it to anyone we wished. The cards were printed with several statements that gave the sender the option of choosing a response: "I (am) (am not) well," or, "I (am) (am not) working." The cards provided a line for the sender's signature, then concluded by stating "I am with a friend

_____."

We left the cards with our captors, who proved not to be in too much of a hurry to dispatch them to their destinations. We turned the cards over to the Japanese about October 1, 1942. My mother received a telephone call from the Wichita Falls postmaster late in the day on Christmas Eve, 1943, informing her that the card had just arrived there. He personally drove to my parents' home to deliver this, the first definite word they had received that I still was alive.

On October 3, 1942, nearly seven months after our capture, the first of our group marched out of Bicycle Camp and boarded a Japanese ship, the *Kinkon Maru*, heading to sea for what turned out to be Singapore. This group, known as "Black Force," consisted of about two hundred Americans and six hundred Australians under the command of Australian Lt. Col. C. M. Black.

The remaining four hundred or so of us joined hundreds of Australian and Dutch POWs and became known as "Burma Railroad Party Branch Five." We left Java on October 11, aboard the *Dai Nichi Maru*, a dirty little tramp steamer that was typical of the Japanese merchant fleet. This group was commanded by Australian Brigadier A. L. Varley, and included our own commanding officer, Lieutenant Colonel Tharp.

Prisoners were crammed by the hundreds in the holds of these ancient, rusting vessels known appropriately as "hell ships." We were so crowded that we had to lie down in shifts. The holds sweltered as the tropical sun beat down relentlessly on metal decks. We were without sufficient food or water, and had no toilets. It was our introduction to the hell on earth that would play out in a ceaseless nightmare awaiting us in the hostile jungles of Burma and Thailand.

6.

Singapore Gathering

THE TRIP TO SINGAPORE aboard the *Dai Nichi Maru* unfolded like a bad dream that lingered on. It took five days from our boarding in Java until, with a collective sigh of relief, we unloaded at the Singapore docks. But those five days seemed interminable. As we mounted the walkway from the dock in Java, the Japs kept up a continuous screeching and yelling to hurry us on.

The *Dai Nichi Maru* itself at first appeared to be in fairly good shape, although it was a smallish vessel that normally hauled supplies — sacked grain, dried vegetables, and rice. As we were herded into the bowels of the ship, with the ever-present guards haranguing and shoving, and occasionally prodding with their rifles, we got a glimpse of our "cruise" quarters. We didn't much like what we saw.

The section immediately below the deck had been subdivided into spaces four to five feet high, and it was into these stalls that we were jammed. Most of us were about six feet tall, and were quite unable to stand in such cramped quarters. We were so crowded that we had to sleep in shifts, some of us sitting in a space about two feet by two feet, so others could stretch out and attempt a few hours of troubled rest.

The journey from Java to Singapore crossed the equator, and the heat in the foul ship became almost unbearable. Had we not still been in fairly good health, little doubt exists that a good number of us would have been dead upon reaching our destination. During the crossing, somebody broke into a closed-off section near where we were quartered and discovered a large quantity of dried potatoes. We nibbled on this God-sent treasure throughout the trip, staving off the worst of hunger.

The only time we were allowed to leave the hold was when we lined up twice daily for our cup of rice, or when we could convince the guard at the top of our quarters that we were on the verge of an uncontrollable bowel movement. A canvas had been strung along one side rail of the top deck as a toilet, and we were allowed to hang our behinds over the side for relief.

The cross-water trip from Java took three days, but our agony aboard the *Dai Nichi Maru* continued on for two more days, as we were forced to languish in the suffocating oven of the hold. Finally we were ordered off, and the excitement at what spread before us lifted our spirits somewhat.

This was romantic Singapore, the great British fortress said to be impregnable to enemy assault. Welcome to one of the queen cities of the East, home of the famous Raffles Hotel, once the Far East residence of noted British authors, site of the Singapore Sling cocktail, first concocted in 1915 by bartender Ngiam Pong Boon. But alas, our dreams of a stay in the Raffles Hotel were not to be fulfilled. Neither had been the boasts of the survivability of Singapore itself, as its "impregnability" was derived solely from assumptions of assault from the sea.

Our eyes strained to see everything about us. The exotic sights, sounds, and smells of this mysterious Oriental island city took our little band of Texans from every side, overwhelming us with new sensations. One of the vividly enduring images from that first glimpse of Singapore is the sight of the stout Chinese coolie women who toiled on and around the docks. Even after a half-century one image is still so vivid that it seems I behold the very act and not the memory: it is a crew of these women rowing a large canoe-shaped boat through the nearby bay as we staggered across the docks, laden with all our earthly possessions, weak from hunger and the heat of the ship's bowels. Later the British told us, to illustrate the toughness of these women, that some had been known to give birth while working, take a ten-minute break, and then return to work. A fantastic story, but some of these women appeared capable of such a performance.

After unloading and going through innumerable *tinkos* or nose counts, to be sure none had escaped, we loaded our possessions on our backs and headed west. On this particular group tour, our "escorts" did not bother with the usual tourist's orientation on Singapore. Instead, with their customary screeching of *"Speedo! Speedo!"* we were hustled aboard trucks and shuttled out to the west side of the island to Camp Changi, a large British military post that had been converted into a prison camp of relative luxury. Our Party Branch Five group arrived at Changi on October 16, 1942, two days after the departure of the Black Force, which already was on its way to Thailand to begin work on the Death Railway.

Those of us left in Changi had what turned out to be three months of rest and relaxation, courtesy of the British Army. The Japanese were most surprised when the British surrendered Singapore with its large army virtually intact. The conquerors were totally unprepared to administer such a large force of prisoners. Consequently, they left the British where they had been before the war, with British officers in charge of the camp's daily routine. There were no Japanese guards inside the sprawling compound. Japanese guards patrolled the gates leading to and from the facility, and the roads around it, but none ventured inside the sprawling compound. They remained conspicuously absent as long as order was maintained inside the camp.

Upon reaching the entrance to Changi, we unloaded the trucks and marched into the camp. Our group, consisting of both army men from the 2d Battalion and survivors of the *Houston,* who had by now melded into a single unit, was housed in a large, two-story building. The British, still maintaining the camp as they had before Nippon came, left us pretty well to ourselves.

We settled in, each finding space to spread his blanket on concrete floors. I managed to work my way onto the kitchen staff, perhaps due to the great depth of my experience in kitchen police duty. Our food at Changi, while a mere shadow of what we had been accustomed to back home, nonetheless proved almost adequate. Bartering for supplemental foods was easy, since the British still had a good supply of their prewar rations.

The British modus operandi at Changi never ceased to amaze us; it was here that some of our group developed an aversion to English military customs. The proper "Limey" officer still had a personal bat-boy — usually a private who served as a personal servant. All the thousands of British troops — both officers and "other ranks" — were required to maintain proper uniforms, and they seemed to have an endless supply of them. They insisted on being properly saluted and given the respect due an officer and gentleman in "His Majesty's Forces." We ridiculed them behind their backs, but managed to avoid personal contact with them for much of our short stay at Changi.

Our second Christmas away from home — and the first in captivity — was spent at Changi. The kitchen crew went all-out for the holiday and prepared a sumptuous meal with some real meat and a fair supply of vegetables. We even had rice pudding for desert.

Someone on the kitchen staff managed to acquire a quantity of gin on Christmas evening. Even now its origin remains a mystery, but probably someone filched it from the Limies. Certainly no one questioned the source, and that evening we threw a party, most of us achieving a state of considerable inebriation. Judging by the number and severity of hangovers the next morning, it was a successful party.

New Year's Day, 1943, found us making ready for the next phase of this sojourn. Word came that within a matter of days we were to be shipped out, our destination somewhere north of Singapore. Before our departure, however, one of my Headquarters Battery friends, Dempsey Key, had spotted a luscious stalk of bananas growing on a tree in the tiny back yard of a British officer's hut.

"We've got to have these bananas," Key said to me one night after we had cleaned up after the evening meal.

"How do you think we can do that?" I asked, my voice trembling with anticipation.

"That's no problem," Key replied. "We simply wait until it is dark and go steal them."

This did not greatly appeal to me; we had observed how tough the British officers were on enlisted men who got even a little bit out of line. But Key was convincing, and the thought of a whole stalk of bananas sent saliva drooling down my chin.

Finally I consented, and Key decided that we would launch our "Operation Rescue Banana" just before midnight.

The night was pitch dark, and we quietly sneaked across an open space where the British often put their troops through close-order drills, and then moved silently to the line of British officers' huts.

As we wiggled our way to a small fence that surrounded the target, it quickly became obvious that snitching the bananas was not going to be a snap. The banana tree looked to be at least ten feet tall, and the objects of our affection hung a good six feet off the ground.

I whispered into Key's ear: "What's the plan? How are we going to do this?"

"You squat down and let me get on your shoulders," he hissed back under his breath.

I got down on my knees and Key placed his legs around my neck. With considerable struggling and muffled grunting, I stood up and slowly walked both of us over to the tree. Key leaned over the little fence, while I struggled to keep my legs from buckling. After what seemed an eternity, he quietly cut the stalk from the banana tree.

I collapsed to the ground and Key tumbled over me, but managed to hold onto the stalk of bananas. We scurried from the area, escaping with the fruit. The stalk furnished us with delicious, ripe bananas for the next two weeks, and proved to be more than worth the risk it took to secure them.

On January 9, 1943, we marched out of the main gate at Changi and proceeded down a long, sloping road toward downtown Singapore. We were guided to the vicinity of Singapore's ornate railway station, where we were herded into small, Asian, metal boxcars which served as our prison for the next few days. The Japanese guards forced about thirty POWs into each car, mercilessly jamming us together. This was no scenic tour we were about to undertake.

The boxcars were about eight feet wide by some twenty feet long, giving each person less than five square feet. The tropical sun transformed the cars into ovens, and we were forced to stay in them for what seemed like hours. Sweat ran from every pore.

Finally, our train crawled out of the station, moved across the half-mile bridge that spans the bay separating Singapore from the mainland, and headed north up the Malay Peninsula.

Few people greeted us as we moved up the peninsula. These people already had been under the heel of the Imperial Japanese Army for a year, and had learned to stay away from places where its soldiers congregated. So there were no friendly, waving natives as our wood-burning train moved us ever closer to our destination.

While the trip seemed to go on and on, the jammed cars were almost bearable as long as the train continued to move and circulate air through them. We managed to urinate from one of the open doors, and since there were fairly frequent stops, one could steal a quickie bowel movement occasionally. But some of our group already suffered from intestinal disorders, and the results caused our close quarters to become even more unbearable.

It took more than forty-eight hours to reach the town of Penang, on Malaya's west coast. The train crawled into what appeared to be a suburban substation. As it jerked to a stop we spilled out of our boxcars and breathed deeply the clean, fresh air moving inland from the nearby sea. As we hit the ground, our guards began yelling barbaric epithets and herded us toward the Penang docks.

"Oh, no!" someone in back of me groaned. "Not another ship trip. This is too much."

But a ship it was. With the usual yells of *"Speedo! Speedo!,"* our keepers herded us aboard another dandy little Japanese tramp steamer. This one was the *Dai Moji Maru,* which turned out to be somewhat larger than the vessel that took us from Java to Singapore. The extra space allowed a small measure of comfort denied us on the voyage of three months earlier. We prepared for another of those testy little cruises sponsored by the Imperial Japanese Army, but as it turned out, this one in the end almost brought us face to face with the bottom of the ocean.

The *Dia Moji Maru,* a vessel of about three thousand tons, steamed out of Penang early on the morning of January 11, 1943, accompanied by another larger vessel. Our naval escort consisted of a tiny corvette that appeared to be an old pleasure yacht armed with a three-inch gun mounted astern. The significance of the escort went unnoticed at the time, but in retrospect illustrated the value the Japanese placed on their human cargo.

The vessels pointed northwest and slowly moved up the Strait of Malacca. The potent tropical sun served as a constant reminder that the area is only a few degrees north of the equator. As the *Dai Moji Maru* crawled toward Burma, our hosts left the coverings off the holds and we managed to pass the time in a state approaching POW elegance. Most of the time was spent lounging in the holds, reading, or playing cards.

I had begun to enjoy the challenge of bridge and was about to launch into a round in which my partner and I had won a bidding war of four hearts, when we were interrupted by a sudden scurrying of feet on the steel deck above.

"I think we'd better put playing this hand off for a while," I told my partner anxiously. At about that time we could hear the low rumble of approaching aircraft. As they grew closer it became obvious that they were the type that normally carry bombs. Someone yelled that they were American bombers, and cold chills ran up my spine. My heart jumped and began to pound as if it would split my chest. We were about to experience our first bombing attack by our own people. It was January 15, 1943, the fourth day of our voyage on the *Dai Moji Maru*.

There are a number of versions of this bombing raid, but my recollection is that the attacking force consisted of two American B-24 Liberators on an enemy ship hunting mission. They had found us, and immediately proceeded to see how many bombs they could place down our smokestacks. The larger ship, the *Nitimei Maru*, was the initial target, and both bombers directed their attention to it. We could hear the distinctive "swoosh" followed by loud explosions as bomb after bomb landed on and around our sister vessel. Several direct hits tore the ship apart, and it was headed for the depths of the Gulf of Martaban in a matter of minutes.

With that task accomplished, the two Liberators turned on the *Dai Moji Maru*. Japanese guards had kept us in the holds at gunpoint, and we huddled there, gripped in fear. Being bombed at sea is one of the most helpless experiences imaginable. The target is precisely and indisputably the very ship which is your temporary shelter. I closed my eyes tightly and wrapped myself in a fetal position, my arms entwined tightly about my head. Never had I known such fear. Being bombed anywhere is bad enough, but at sea it is the worst of ordeals. There's no running, no escape.

The first bomber made a run at our vessel and dropped two bombs which straddled it amidships. Both were near misses, but the bombs, as they exploded in the sea, sent an avalanche of water over us. Shrapnel tore several holes in the metal sides. Meanwhile, the Japanese crew were firing surface guns fore and aft, with absolutely no results — they were designed for ground, not air targets. The ship's guns managed only some self-inflicted damage and failed utterly to interfere with the mission of the aircraft. A shot from the forward gun apparently hit a steel cable that stretched across an area near the bridge, and the exploding shell ripped a corner from the structure in which the crew conned the ship.

The rear gun suffered a breach explosion on its third or fourth firing, the blast killing most of the Japanese gun crew along with several Australian prisoners of war huddled on the deck nearby. This mishap set off a small fire on the back deck of the ship, causing some consternation until it was brought under control.

In its turn, the second Liberator made a run on us and dropped two bombs that barely missed each side of the fantail. The explosions inflicted considerably more damage, since the bombs appeared to fall closer than their earlier companions. The *Dai Moji Maru* captain was zigzagging frantically, trying to escape the bombs. The Liberators seemed to have nearly expended their bombs on the larger ship and must have had only two left apiece when they turned on us. This undoubtedly saved many lives; we were forty-eight miles from Moulmein, Burma, our destination, and few of us, if any, could have swum that far.

The bombers finally left. Our ship returned to where the other vessel had sunk and began picking up survivors. One bomb apparently scored a direct hit on the compartment where about five hundred Japanese engineers and other personnel were housed. It reportedly killed most of the enemy, and eventually delayed our task of beginning work on the Death Railway. In addition to the Japanese casualties, almost fifty Dutch POWs lost their lives. We hovered in the area for two or three hours, picking up nearly eight hundred Dutch POWs and some two hundred Japanese civilians en route to Burma to supervise the construction of the Death Railroad. I vividly recall watching one Dutchman covered with blood crawl up a rope ladder from the sea to the deck of our ship. Just after reaching the deck, he collapsed and died from stomach wounds that exposed most of his entrails.

The additional thousand passengers placed a strain on space in our ship. Completing the task of picking up survivors, the *Dai Moji Maru* turned back toward Burma. Just after we got underway again, I had the misfortune of standing on deck close to a Japanese guard who, when he determined that I was an American, took his frustration out on me. He used his rifle to jam me in the stomach repeatedly, then turned the butt of the rifle and slugged me in the head. I thought he was going to kill me, and he may have done so, had not a Japanese sergeant intervened. The noncommissioned officer sent the guard away and left me lying on the deck nursing my wounds. Fortunately, the attack had not broken any bones, and being only twenty years old at the time and still in fair physical shape, I recovered in a day or so.

There was little rest or sleep during the night as we slowly moved toward land. Early on the morning of January 16, we entered the dirty waters of the Salween River that serve as the port for the city of Moulmein. Before we unloaded on floating piers, there was another airplane scare. A Japanese bomber approached the area, creating panic. Two prisoners jumped overboard and started swimming toward the banks. Guards fired several shots in front of them, and they turned back toward the ship and were picked up.

The ever-present, searing tropical sun beat down unmercifully as we unloaded on the floating docks. A large statue of Buddha perched atop a nearby hill overlooking the wide, brown river stared impassively out to sea. Someone started quoting Rudyard Kipling's *On the Road to Mandalay,* and the passage about the golden pagoda: "the dawn came up like thunder over Moulmein across the bay."

We marched through the near-deserted city to a red brick prison surrounded by high walls, where we spent the next five days. Also housed in the prison were native convicted felons. Twice a day we watched these convicts, shackled leg to leg, take a few minutes' break in the open air. Their brief walk was carried out in extreme difficulty since the heavy chains allowed only slow, laborious movement. Finally, we had encountered someone whose status was even lower than our own.

Food and water were in shorter supply in the Moulmein prison, and some of the group came down with dysentery, the wracking bowel disease that was to become commonplace later in the jungles. As bad as these conditions seemed, however, the time was fast approaching when that short interlude where we slept on concrete floors would be remembered as not exactly pleasant, but infinitely preferable.

7.

To Work We Go

JANUARY 21, 1943, found us again packing our meager possessions and marching out of the Moulmein prison. We walked
through the town, which still appeared virtually deserted, to the
nearby railway station. There we boarded more small, hot, Asian
boxcars for a thirty-mile journey to the town of Thanbyuzayat,
the staging area for the northern end of the Death Railway.

Thanbyuzayat is located on a broad plain flanked on three
sides by mountains. A bamboo fence separated the newer section,
where Japanese staff and guards were quartered, from the larger
area where prisoners were kept. It was our first experience with
the long, barn-like bamboo structures that would be our POW
homes for the nearly three years of captivity stretching before us.
The structures usually were about twenty-five feet wide and several hundred feet long. Bamboo poles of varying sizes were used
for framing. The roof consisted of dried leaves woven into one-by-
three-foot sections which overlapped to form a supposedly water-
tight canopy against the coming monsoon.

A three-foot-high section of woven split bamboo served as
the only siding for the huts. Inside, an aisle about three feet wide
separated platforms on either side where the occupants lived and
slept. These platforms were about three feet above the ground
and were made from split bamboo, fastened together with green
fibers similar to grapevines.

Our stay at Thanbyuzayat was not a long one, but several memorable events keep this, our first camp on the railroad, etched in my mind. Shortly after debarking from the train, we marched into camp. Leaving our gear in our assigned spaces, we assembled on the adjacent, dusty parade ground. Lieutenant Colonel Nagatomo, Japanese commander of Branches Three and Five work forces, strutted, samurai sword at his side, to a platform in a preview of things to come. After uttering a series of glowing praises for the Emperor, Nagatomo, in his high-pitched, sing-song voice, addressed the prisoners before him:

> You are only a few remaining skeletons after the invasion of East Asia [by the Western civilizations] for the past few centuries, and are pitiful victims. It is not your fault, but until your governments wake up from their dreams and discontinue their resistance, all of you will not be released. However, I shall not treat you badly for the sake of humanity as you have no fighting power left at all.

His voice rose shrilly as he praised the "inestimable thoughts and infinite favors of His Imperial Majesty," telling us we should "weep with gratitude at the greatness of them." Then, stating his desire to correct our "misleading and improper anti-Japanese ideas," he declared:

> We will build the railroad if we have to build it over the white man's body. It gives me great pleasure to have a fast-moving defeated nation in my power. You are merely rubble but I will not feel bad because it is [the fault of] your rulers. If you want anything, you will have to come through me . . . and there will be many of you who will not see your homes again. Work cheerfully at my command.

Then, after warning that any attempt to escape would be met with execution, the pint-sized colonel told us what an honor it was to be involved in the important task of linking Thailand and Burma by a rail line. He concluded by ordering us to work earnestly and confidently, swaggered to his nearby automobile and was driven away in a cloud of dust.

We stood on the hot, dry parade ground, silent and stunned by the words of this enemy officer. He had hurled a series of orders and threats at us, none designed to assure our well-being. His speech had rambled and carried some inconsistencies, but many of his threats proved prophetic.

Several months earlier, the Japanese had established a headquarters in Kanburi, Thailand, to direct the railway construction project. Japanese units engaged in the work were known as the Southern Army Railway Corps, consisting of the 5th Regiment, based in Thanbyuzayat, and the 9th in Kanburi. Altogether, the Japanese had about 12,000 men employed in the project, and work was to proceed from both ends of the proposed railway, from Thanbyuzayat in the north, south to Ban Pong, Thailand, where the line joined the existing Thai railway system.

Before leaving Thanbyuzayat for our first work camp, the Japanese brought in a supply of anti-cholera vaccine, one of the few times our captors showed any concern for our health. Perhaps they were trying to preserve as many of us as possible until they could finish the railroad. We lined up and Lt. Cmdr. W. A. Epstein, the *Houston*'s medical officer, and other medical personnel administered the vaccine. When he got to me, Dr. Epstein pushed the dull needle into my left arm, only to discover that the vaccine supply was exhausted. He detached the empty cylinder, leaving the needle in my arm, refilled it, reattached it to the needle, and finished giving me the shot.

A week later we boarded Japanese trucks and were driven to our work station, designated 18 Kilo Camp because it was eighteen kilometers from Thanbyuzayat, where the new line began. It was a typical work camp, located alongside the railroad at the edge of the jungle. Each of these camps consisted of three to five acres and usually housed from two to five thousand prisoners.

To the rest of the world it was January 25, 1943. To us, it was the day the easy life ended.

8.

The Jungle

OUR FIRST WORK camp, 18 Kilo, perched on the very edge of the jungle. Upon arrival there, we gazed in wonder at the thick, trackless tangle of endless rows of trees which appeared locked together in a blanket of undergrowth defying penetration.

We trudged through hot, humid tropical air into the camp and wearily sought our assigned huts. Each man was allotted a space about three feet wide and six feet long. After unloading our gear, we stood outside the bamboo buildings contemplating the immediate future. Even at this point, many — most — of us failed to realize how bad things were to become, but apprehension gripped us as we gazed into the Burma jungle, destined to be the last place hundreds of our men would ever see in this world.

We were organized into groups according to our nationality, and then subdivided into working gangs which the Japanese called *"Kumis."* Americans were a minority in all of these camps, with the bulk of prisoners being Dutch, Australians, or British. The day after our arrival at 18 Kilo Camp, all *Kumis* were moved out of the camp, going to either end of the line to begin work.

Each *Kumi* had its own officer who acted as foreman and was assigned a Japanese guard. The foreman served under direct command of Japanese engineer officers. Most of the guards were Koreans, who had been conscripted by the Japanese and assigned the lowest tasks in the army. The Japanese considered the

71

Koreans subhuman, often beating them unmercifully. The Korean guards, in turn, inflicted similar punishment on the prisoners, often battering them senseless for the least infraction. The lack of a common language often led to misunderstandings, which in turn led to lashings and beatings.

At the beginning, each working POW was assigned the task of moving one cubic meter of earth daily, and received a holiday every tenth day. Many of us were without the luxury of mosquito nets; it was only a matter of time before malaria began taking its toll. Hard work, inadequate food (barely sufficient to keep one alive), and few or no medical supplies hastened the spread of disease throughout the work force. Those who became ill, but who could still rise and work, were assigned light duty; this allowed most *Kumis* to meet their work quota.

It was hot, but still dry. The monsoon was yet three months in the future, and would descend upon us as we worked our way deeper into the jungles. Our food was nearly adequate – by Japanese standards. Rice was the staple and cattle or swine were sometimes delivered on the hoof. The bulk of our so-called vegetables, however, consisted chiefly of light green melons which one of our Australian cobbers referred to as "water standing up." Our captors "paid" us, when we were able to work, in locally printed occupation money, with privates getting twenty-five cents a day and noncommissioned officers thirty cents.

The Japanese let us establish a canteen in camp and brought in such luxuries as duck eggs, tomatoes, gula (a native-brewed brick of dark sugar), and bulk tobacco. Most of us still smoked, and this "wog" tobacco was wicked indeed. It was so strong that we learned to wash it two or three times, wringing out the dark brown liquid and letting it dry again before turning it into roll-your-own cigarettes. Paper was a rare commodity, and we turned mostly to dried banana leaves. The bulk tobacco would become very dry after its washing, and we learned that banana peels, when they were available, would remoisten the "weed" and even impart a fruity flavor.

Prices at the canteen usually prohibited overindulgence. A duck egg cost one dollar, or four days' pay for a private. A kilogram of the hard sugar cost about four dollars, or half a month's salary. The workers were paid about once every ten days. If one became too ill to work, however, pay was cut off and food rations were reduced. Even through these times of virtual starvation, most of us clung to our smoking habit. I recall inhaling that strong, dark brown bulk tobacco rolled up in a banana leaf and experiencing a sharp stab in my lungs that seemed to ricochet upwards in my throat and bounce off the top of my skull. It was wicked stuff, but we clung to it like a baby clings to a blanket.

March 15, 1943, saw our group packed up and loaded onto Japanese trucks — some of them fueled by wood-burning stoves — and hauled deep into the jungles to a newly established camp at 85 Kilo. This camp was at the end of the cleared area, and was located in rugged, heavily wooded hills that made our work harder. It was at this point that our American group suffered its first death, and the loss had a profound effect on our small party. Marine Sgt. J. M. Lusk, who had survived the sinking of the *Houston* a year earlier, had been suffering from severe attacks of malaria. His condition was probably worsened by dysentery and beriberi, and on March 22, 1943, while still at 80 Kilo, he died. Lusk was a big, barrel-chested Marine, seemingly indestructible. His death was a shock, but only a prelude to the avalanche of fatalities soon to crash down upon us.

Our stay at 85 Kilo was short-lived, and in early April we again rolled up our meager belongings and walked the five kilometers back to 80 Kilo. This camp was in a small, sunken valley surrounded by huge forests of bamboo which cut off any breeze trying to penetrate the area. Most of the POWs began to fall victim to dysentery, beriberi, and general weakness from malnutrition. It was at this point that tropical ulcers began to add to our misery. Huge, black sores that usually develop when a scratch or cut becomes infected, the ulcers spread rapidly, and within three to four days could multiply in size ten times over. They usually occurred around the feet and legs, which were more susceptible to injury during heavy manual labor. Most of us by this time had no shoes or boots, and had to work barefoot. The ulcers could spread over one's legs and feet, exposing bones and even causing toes to drop off.

Within weeks of our arrival at 80 Kilo, heavy clouds began

building over the jungles. It was obvious that the rains were not far off. Initially, we welcomed the rain as a relief from the wretched heat that sapped what little strength we had left. The deluge quickly drowned our joy. The monsoon had matured by the end of May. With the rains, sickness increased, leading to more deaths. Frequently, half the work force was incapacitated by disease, and we began falling behind in our work. The Japanese started keeping us out on the job until after dark. By the end of May, it was usually midnight before we stumbled into our camp almost unconscious from exhaustion after eighteen continuous hours of labor on the railroad.

On many occasions during this period, I recall dragging my exhausted, emaciated body to that split bamboo bed and actually falling asleep before my head touched the platform. My Christian faith, adopted while a young teenager, deepened. I prayed diligently. While reciting these prayers, I acknowledged to God that I was in much trouble and helpless to influence my situation personally. I asked the Creator for protection and expressed my desire to survive my plight and return home. I concluded by affirming that if it were not the will of God that I should survive, I would accept whatever fate He had for me. During these days of eighteen hours' toil on the railroad, I often fell asleep before praying. Almost without exception, I would awaken and immediately realize that I had not prayed. After performing my nightly ritual, I would instantly fall asleep again.

A medium-sized river wound its way through the jungles near 80 Kilo Camp, and we spent several weeks working on a large, double-decked bridge spanning it. We gathered large pilings for the bridge from the ample supply of jungle trees, stripping their limbs and toting them to the bridge site. The Japanese had us construct a scaffold perhaps thirty feet tall, using large bamboo or small trees. This scaffold, held together by ropes and a few bolts, became the "machine" used to drive the piling into the ground for the bridge base. A hole about three inches in diameter was drilled in one end of a piling and a long, round iron bar inserted into the hole. A bell-shaped weight of several hundred pounds with a hole in the center was inserted onto the iron bar. A big rope threaded through a pulley wheel was tied to the bell-shaped weight and reached back to the ground where the pile-driving crew awaited. A dozen or more small ropes were attached to the big rope, and the POW crew each grabbed a rope, pulled the weight six to eight feet up the iron bar and let it drop, driving the pile into the ground.

A Japanese engineer would count cadence for the pile drivers. From the time of Bicycle Camp, our captors had made us learn basic commands — attention, about face, forward march, and so forth — in Japanese. By 1943, we grasped the rudiments of it and the Javanese that inevitably worked its way into our composite language. I still clearly recall the engineer's sing-song voice yelling, *"Ichi, ni, no san, yon!"* Clunk![1] By this method, we constructed a long, curving, double-decked bridge across this deep, swift river. Several workers lost their lives on the bridge in falls or other accidents. And it was here that I suffered two small abrasions on my right leg that later ulcerated, almost killing me.

Typically, each working camp was assigned two dozen Japanese army guards who lived in camp with us, although they were segregated in their own area with quarters substantially better than those of the POWs. For the most part, the same guards stayed with us until the railroad was completed.

Our guards varied in temperament. Some were tolerant, some were bad, and a few were barbaric — at the blink of an eye they would club you with a rifle or anything else within reach. The Koreans, as a group, were the worst of the lot. The Japanese considered themselves superior to the Koreans, and to all white men in general. They appeared to particularly despise the Koreans and rarely let pass an opportunity to zap one.

Since these Korean guards bore the brunt of Japanese abuse, they in turn took their frustrations out on us. We were subjected to frequent and sometimes violent punishment. Using our wit — the only weapon we possessed — to get back at our tormentors, we gave the guards nicknames. One of the Koreans apparently had suffered a severe smallpox attack earlier in life, and he soon became known to the POWs as "Pock." Perhaps the most vicious,

---

1. "One, two, and a three, four!"

and surely the dumbest, of the Korean guards was a big fellow who stood over six feet tall and had a large, round head and fat lips. He was soon awarded the moniker, "Liver Lips."

Liver Lips had a vile temper and was among the ugliest of God's men. He must have weighed well over two hundred pounds. His huge head and round face featured a big, flat nose and dark brown, beady eyes. He was something of a loner, since even his fellow Koreans appeared to avoid his company.

None of the guards spoke or understood English, so at times we would have a little fun with some of them. Occasionally, when things were going well and most of us, including our guard, were in good humor, one of us would strike up a "conversation" with the guard. The POW would grin broadly and start saying in a very friendly voice, "Hello, you ugly son of a bitch! I bet you were hatched somewhere under a rock." The uncomprehending guard would grin back and assume a friendly manner, apparently under the impression that the prisoners were giving him a compliment.

One day on a work project Liver Lips was assigned to our *Kumi*. During one of two ten-minute breaks allowed us, some of our group walked to a nearby cluster of trees to urinate. As they rounded the clump, they came upon Liver Lips in the process of masturbating. He looked up and saw the POWs watching and roared like a wounded bull. The POWs scattered like a covey of quail, but the damage had been done. In short order everybody in the camp heard the story of Liver Lips' indiscretion and in coming weeks, if any of us even looked at him he would bellow and often club the offender with his rifle. He remained in a vile temper for weeks, and we soon learned to make a wide detour when he was in the vicinity.

Weeks into our work at 80 Kilo, a new guard was assigned to our *Kumi*. He was quite young, probably no more than sixteen or seventeen. A small man, he initially appeared to be very timid. One day while we were hauling trees from the jungle to a bridge site, the youngster was "guarding" us and we decided on our own to take a rest. At first the little guard just stood there looking confused. But he soon decided it was time to assert his authority, and started yelling at us. His yelling, however, came out in high-pitched squeaks, and we all burst into laughter. He stood there, momentarily in confusion, but apparently having a pretty good sense of humor, joined us in laughter. We laughed for some time — there was so little to laugh about. Finally, our small guard sat down on the log with us and we relaxed for about ten minutes. Soon we got up and resumed our work. From that time on, this little guard was friendly with us and rarely lashed out as others often did.

The monsoon was in full bloom by the end of May as we finished work on the railway bed around the 80 Kilo section. At the other end of the rail line a few dozen of our fellow American POWs had joined British and Australians in Thailand, and were working northward toward where our own crews had steadily cut into the jungles from the opposite direction. Some of the Thai camps were even worse, if that was possible, than ours in Burma. Nevertheless, in both Burma and Thailand, disease and death became commonplace by the end of May 1943.

On May 29, 1943, we loaded our worldly possessions on our backs and were forced to march down a jungle road twenty kilometers to what was to be the infamous 100 Kilo Camp. Much of this march was through ankle-deep mud, one of the blessings of the rainy season. The long march must have taken us some twenty-four hours or more, although to this day I do not recall if it were day or night when we arrived at 100 Kilo. We already were weak from malnutrition and from debilitating diseases and the strain of overwork. The march was one long blur that even decades later can be recalled only as a nightmare. The weight of our gear became intolerable, and some of us threw away scarce possessions which, at the time, did not seem absolutely necessary for survival.

After we dragged our near-lifeless bodies into 100 Kilo, work *Kumis* resumed. The rain beat down day and night. We often rose well before dawn, had a small bowl of rice, and marched out to our assigned work site. Our slave drivers would dictate the quota of work for that day, and we toiled, often well into the night, until that quota was completed.

Anyone who has ridden a train or even seen a railroad running ribbon-like through the countryside knows that the railway bed must be as level as possible. Inclines and declines must not be at too steep a grade or the train will either fail to climb or will descend too fast. Thus, to build a new railroad bed, low places must be filled, and high places must be shaved. The enormous amount of work necessary to build a 260-mile railroad through untrekked jungles, over seemingly endless rolling hills and mountains, across uncounted valleys and through thick, trackless jungles, defies the imagination. Rivers and streams must be bridged, and virtually all of this work was done by human labor, in the age-old Asian custom. Correspondingly, at about the time of our arrival in Burma in early 1943, the Japanese combed the countryside and "recruited" about 270,000 Chinese, Malays, Tamils, and other native laborers from Burma, Malaya, and Thailand to work with some 60,000 Allied POWs on the railroad.

Work on the first fifty to seventy kilometers of the railway extending southeast from Thanbyuzayat was relatively easy — that section lay over fairly level ground. But near 80 Kilo Camp, we reached the rivers. And we reached the mountains. Our only tools were picks, shovels, and a few sledgehammers. To move the tons of earth needed to fill the depressions, we used two ancient Asian devices, a two-man litter comprising two poles and a bamboo mat, and a one-man "yo-yo pole" with bamboo baskets suspended from each end.

With iron and bamboo we were given a year to move and shape 4 million cubic meters of earth, 3 million cubic meters of rock, and build fourteen kilometers of bridges.

Urged on by a Japanese slave-master, each *Kumi* of about fifty men did essentially three things: fill depressions with basket after basket of earth, cut through the dirt and rock of hills and mountains, and bridge the streams and rivers that drained the jungle. To the uninitiated, the daily quota of one cubic meter of earth moved per man per day may not seem significant, but it proved torturously difficult — and it would soon increase.

As the work moved from the plains deeper into the jungle, rolling hills became small mountains. The mountains had to be pierced. Their foundations of rock yielded to the dynamite of the

Japanese engineers. Then the prisoners went in, wearily swinging the sledgehammers that would smash the shattered boulders into gravel for the railroad bed. Some of the dirt and gravel became fill for depressions.

The mountains had no end. Bodies wasted and minds stupefied, we thought only of getting through the next minute. The Japanese urged us, hounded us, but we worked to survive only; our effort was just enough to avoid a bashing.

The hardest labor was in swinging the pick to break up the earth. *Kumis* swapped off about every two hours — as much as our sapped bodies could stand. But Charley Pryor, a Marine survivor of the *Houston,* allowed no substitution. He later recalled having never used anything but the pick. He was a strapping six feet, two inches, and swung the pick like it was a toy.

The Japanese exhibited great skill at building bridges from mostly native material. After they selected a crossing site, we were put to work felling trees and carrying them to the location. A moderately large bridge required several hundred logs. That meant long, weary days of cutting down trees and hauling them, sometimes over hundreds of yards, occasionally with the help of elephants. When sufficient logs were on hand for piling, we cut smaller logs for bracing. Then came timber for the pile-driver scaffolding, and the serious work of bridge-building was underway.

Going from making fills and cuts to building bridges brought no relief. Felling the large trees selected by the Japanese engineer, trimming them limbless, and carrying them to the bridge site was back-breaking work. Trees selected for the bridges were a type of hardwood. Some were so heavy that the elephants working on our detail refused to carry them. But the elephants always carried authority. A crew of eight to ten POWs had to match the elephant's pace; when it insisted on a break, however, the men continued working alone.

On one site, our elephant, whose driver was a Burmese boy about twelve years old, had worked steadily for hours when he stopped and refused to continue. One of our POW crew walked slowly to within a few feet of the elephant and yelled, "Get to work! If we have to do it, you have to do it!"

That was enough for the elephant. Hurling his trunk back over his head, he trumpeted and charged the POW. He shoved the man to the ground, imprisoning him on either side with his tusks, and glared down with hateful eyes, less than a foot from the man's face.

We stood transfixed as the elephant vented his fury. His tantrum lasted minutes which seemed like hours. Then he raised his head from the petrified prisoner, shook it from side to side, turned, and contemptuously strolled back to his chores. We did not bother him again.

Early in 1943, the war began to turn against the Japanese. They grew desperate to finish the Siam-Burma railroad. The original November completion date was accelerated to August. The Japanese began their *"Speedo"* campaign, increasing the workload of the POWs and the native laborers past human endurance. The one-meter quota swelled to two and one-half meters. The hounding turned to screaming, guards shrieking *"Speedo! Speedo!"* and waving their fists in the air as we died in the dirt at their feet. We did not meet their hopes. Their railroad would not be finished until late October.

Within a few months after beginning work on the railroad, our clothing began to disintegrate. Soon most of us were without shoes or boots, working in our bare feet. Shirts and trousers became scarce. Some prisoners sold their clothes to natives, others began cutting up their rags to make g-strings, a piece of cloth about a foot wide and a yard long. On one end of the cloth, a drawstring encircled the waist and held the cloth in place. The Japanese provided no clothing, and eventually every POW was forced to wear a g-string.

Before the monsoon began, drinking water was critically short. We worked under the same tropical sun that had broiled us at sea. We were allowed two cups of water to replace the streams that ran from our pores into the soil. By early afternoon, visions of cool water replaced all else. Later, with the monsoon breaking over us in the jungle, water was plentiful. But the deluge brought its own agonies; disease — so often fatal — thrived where nothing ever dried. During the monsoon, our sodden hell ended only when we dragged our exhausted bodies back from the railway to our filthy bunks for a few hours' sleep.

As we advanced into the jungles and mountains, we climbed in altitude and frequently encountered chilly temperatures, with no clothes to warm us. At night, the chill, compounded by lice infestations and disease, led to troubled sleep. Nightmares struck me frequently. I often awoke, shaking uncontrollably in a cold sweat. One particularly dreadful nightmare occurred over and over. I would be asleep on a bamboo mat inside a small, square room. Suddenly, a green-faced figure with a long, pointed nose, black hair, and a sharp chin with a dagger-like beard would stick its head through the door and glare down at me. I was powerless to move and would finally awaken to my own moans. I feared the dream would not relent, but it stopped after I left the jungle.

By early June 1943, virtually everyone was suffering from a host of debilitating diseases. Food became even scarcer as the Japanese began to force more and more work on the prisoners. The monsoon rains fell relentlessly. We arose hours before dawn in a steady rain, ate our meager ration of rice, and trudged off to the work site in a constant steady rain. It was impossible to manage even a few dry minutes. As more and more men became seriously ill and desperately emaciated, the state of agitation among the Japanese grew. Soon, they forced the "light sick" to move out of camp to work sites for "light duty." These men would have been hospitalized in normal times; they were those whose ulcers still allowed them to limp about, or whose dysentery had not yet reached the flood stage, or whose malaria had yet to become critical. Working these sick men pushed many of them directly to their deaths.

Guards assigned to "light duty" working parties often appeared to take it as an insult, and would brutalize their charges. They kicked ulcerated legs, bashed the wretched POWs with rifle butts, or beat them unmercifully with bamboo poles or other weapons close at hand.

As the work grew increasingly burdensome, the food supply became critically short. Often the narrow dirt road used by trucks to bring in supplies to the work camps washed out, delaying delivery of the meager rations. We trudged to work and back to camp in the dark, often in a daze of confusion. Exhaustion gripped our minds and bodies, and our eviscerated lives seemed to drag on minute by minute, hour by hour. It became impossible to remember what day of the week it was, or even what month.

Along with our strength our compassion shriveled; we could manage barely enough for our own number. One day my *Kumi* was hauling rock from a site in the nearby jungle to cover completed railway beds. Our Japanese engineer had some dynamite to blast apart the larger stone formations, which we were assigned to further crush to surface the railway bed. The engineer set his charge, lit the fuse and we all scurried for cover. We waited. Nothing happened. In a few minutes, the Jap stuck his head over a boulder and decided the fuse had gone out. He got up, and headed for the blast site, when suddenly it exploded. The engineer was killed by the blast, and we were sent back to camp early. None of us felt sorry for the poor fellow; he was one of the more aggressive of our captors and often beat prisoners to force more work from them.

On another occasion, our work party was returning to camp before dark. On our way, we came upon a sleeping Burmese native who had a pair of oxen. This was too great a temptation, and our guard agreed to let us attempt to rustle the livestock. One of our group picked up a club and held it above the head of the sleeping Burmese, while others untied the oxen and walked off with them. The Burmese was still asleep when we left, and that evening we had some real, although somewhat tough, meat for our stew.

A few weeks after our arrival at 100 Kilo Camp, I reached the conclusion that doing something other than going out on work parties was essential for my survival. I somehow managed to talk my way onto the kitchen crew, which was exempt from regular labor. During this period, a work party discovered two tiger cubs in the jungle. They could not have been more than a week or two old. They were brought into camp that night and proved to be a very entertaining, but short-lived diversion.

Our kitchen crew had to arise at 3:00 A.M. to cook the morning ration of rice for the *Kumis*. A typical kitchen crew consisted of about six enlisted men, a mess sergeant, and an officer in charge. The meal ration was about a cup of rice per man, which added up to a considerable amount, with the hundreds of mouths for which we cooked. Normally we had about five or six large cast iron pots about a meter in diameter. We placed a measured amount of raw rice in each pot, covered it with water from the nearby creek and built large fires under each cooking vessel. It took half-an-hour's cooking to get the rice to the desired texture, and to kill anything that might be lingering in the water. We used large wooden paddles, similar to oars for a boat, to stir the rice as it bubbled in the *wi-johns*. We served the rice directly from them to individual POWs as they lined up for breakfast. My job consisted of making the fires, occasionally stirring the rice, and helping to ladle it out to the men. When a pot of rice was cooked, there was always a browned layer of it left stuck to the bottom of the vessels. This was "gravy" for the kitchen crew, when we could manage to get our hands on some of it. Most of the browned crust was designated by our camp doctor for the sick and disabled.

One morning, we had just started the cooking fires and filled the large, round pots, when just across the small, nearby creek there came a piercing animal-like scream. One of the Japanese guard posts was in that general area, and within seconds the Jap guard was in our midst jabbering frantically that something was after him. It turned out that the mother tiger had followed the scent of her cubs to the camp and had almost gotten to the guard.

Orders went out to return the tiger cubs to the site where they had been found. The unpleasant task was performed by the men who had abducted them originally, and that was the end of the tiger episode at 100 Kilo Camp.

Alas, my easy job in the kitchen was not to endure. A few weeks after joining the kitchen crew, Lieutenant Keithly, the same Keithly whose shiny boots had been splattered with my vomit back in Java, was assigned duty as kitchen officer. The next day my name was added to the outside work roster, and I was back working on the railroad. This reassignment to the outside work force would soon bring me to the nadir of my life as a POW.

9.

A Place to Die

THE PASSING OF my twenty-first birthday, on July 25, 1943, lies somewhere back in the subconscious that houses volumes of memories which simply refuse to open. The middle months of 1943 are one vague blur of work, fatigue, pain, and suffering. Often we were at the work site for eighteen hours, afterwards dragging our weary, emaciated bodies into camp barely conscious of what was going on around us. One incident stands out, remarkable for the mirth it introduced into what was just another long dreary, deadly session of toil.

At the end of one of the interminable work days, our Japanese guard decided to do something special as we returned to camp. For some forgotten reason, we had completed the day's quota in dirt and rock and were going back "home" before dark.

The Japanese military in these days marched in a "goose step." With a sinister gleam in his eye, our guard halted our detail a few hundred yards from the compound gate and indicated to us through grunts, gestures, and a few words in mixed languages that our weary little band of slaves was to goose step as we marched into camp past the guardhouse entry.

Just out of sight of his fellow guards, our "commander" had us practice a few goose steps without much success. The chaotic result of this drill should have given him ample notice of what was about to take place, but he was determined to show us off.

Just as we rounded a curve leading to the gate entrance, he bellowed the command to goose step, and we started trying to comply. The result was just the opposite of what our guard hoped for. We stumbled and fell over each other and ended in such disorder that the guards at the gate began roaring with laughter, and all of us joined in. It must have looked like something out of Laurel and Hardy. Our guard was so embarrassed that he forgot to punish anybody, and we slouched into camp in our usual unmilitary shuffle. It was the last time a guard tried anything of that nature.

The animation of laughter was a rare thing and we remained bound in the loathsome strands of a web of misery. Lice abounded in the jungle. It is impossible to recall when these hitchhikers first showed on our bodies, but soon after our arrival in Burma in early 1943, they became an ever-present scourge. We probably first came in contact with them at Moulmein where we were housed in that dirty native prison.

Lice must have been dwelling in the cracks of every bamboo building in Burma. They infested what little clothing we had left, hid in our bedding and other gear, and clung to virtually every piece of bamboo used to construct the long, narrow huts in which we lived for the remaining years of our captivity. There was no way to get rid of them; we had no sanitation facilities — often, we went weeks, even months, without a chance to wash even our hands. The Burmese lice were flesh colored and hard to spot unless — as usually happened — a bite triggered an itch that revealed its location. They burrowed into every crack or crevice on the body and fed until double or triple in size.

Lice were the most persistent in the hair of the head, around the waist and in the crotch. I clearly remember watching the Burmese peasants, during their rare leisure moments, search through the thick, dark hair of a friend's or family member's head for the lice that brought misery without regard to race, creed, or color. For many years following our release, the recollection of lice would spur the irresistible urge to scratch.

In late July 1943, the work schedule stretched into one long befogged period of pain, suffering, and endless rain. Sometime during this period the two sores on my right leg, midway between the ankle and knee, began spreading rapidly in every direction and became fully developed tropical ulcers. The two black sores, the result of scratches obtained while working on that big bridge near the 80 Kilo Camp, spread into one long, gory mass of pus and dead flesh, covering the front half of the leg from knee to shin. The disease had eaten away the thin layer of flesh over the leg bone, exposing it in two places. The ulcer dominated my right leg, and soon sapped what little strength I had left in my emaciated body. It gnawed through so much flesh and so many blood vessels that I was forced to keep the leg elevated above my heart to staunch the continuous loss of blood.

A few weeks before I was stricken with this huge ulcer, so many of my fellow POWs had become disabled from various tropical diseases that what to do with them became a major problem. To solve this dilemma and to remove the hopelessly ill from among those still able to work, the Japanese reopened the 80 Kilo Camp as a "hospital." A hospital it was not; it was, in reality, a place to store the skeletal bodies of the desperately ill where they could die in a more "convenient" location.

After first becoming bedridden, I remained flat on my back in my bunk at 100 Kilo while those still able to function went out to work. My pallet, in one of the long bamboo huts, overlooked an open space some fifty to one hundred feet wide that separated it from another building used to house the sick. S. H. Lumpkin of Amarillo, our battalion medical officer, worked virtually around the clock to keep the most gravely ill of our group alive. But death had become common by late July, and Lumpkin began performing autopsies in hopes of gaining some knowledge of these mysterious tropical diseases that lay largely outside his considerable medical knowledge.

The good doctor and his orderly helpers erected a split bamboo platform about waist-high just outside my bunk area. I could easily see over the narrow bamboo mat siding, and often lay there, transfixed, as Lumpkin performed the autopsies. He used a saw to remove the top of a skull so he could examine the brain. He would split open the abdomen and study the stomach and its contents. I must have witnessed a dozen or more of these procedures, and it occurred to me at the time that this experience would be invaluable should he, or any of us, survive this ordeal.

Soon I received word that I was to be transported back to the

80 Kilo hospital. This must have been just before my twenty-first birthday, because I vaguely remember that momentous event passing after my arrival there. A friend, or perhaps one of Dr. Lumpkin's medical orderlies, helped me hobble to a road outside the camp where I lay awaiting a truck headed in the right direction.

It was hot and the sun beat down on me as I lay beside the dusty road, my head resting on my rolled-up bedding. There was no nearby shade, and sweat rolled into my eyes and soaked my ragged shorts around the waist and in the crotch. After languishing there for the better part of an hour, a Japanese officer came up and demanded to know what I was doing. I pointed to the soiled makeshift bandage on my leg and said, *"Bioke! Bioke!"* (Sick! Sick!) then told him that I was awaiting transportation back to 80 Kilo. He wanted to know what was wrong with me — why wasn't I able to work? Again, I pointed to my right leg, swathed from knee to shin in that long strip of dirty bandage.

The enemy officer was becoming increasingly agitated and with arms waving and mouth going a mile a minute, he demanded to see my wounded leg. Slowly I began unwrapping the pus and bloodstained bandage, and instantly the stench of rotting flesh reached his nostrils. He backed away hurriedly, holding his nose, and motioned frantically for me to wrap the rag back over my rotting leg.

The Japanese officer turned his back and scurried away to whatever business he was on, leaving me lying beside the dusty road, awaiting transportation. For once it wasn't raining, and I stretched out on my side and tried to relax my spinning brain. It was hot and humid. Sweat continued streaming down my forehead into my eyes, and my armpits dripped like a leaky bucket. What was going on at this 80 Kilo hospital I was destined for? Every time the subject of this sick camp came up, those who knew what was happening there would clam up and look strained, as if trying to forget something. Finally, after what seemed an interminable period of roadside solitude, a truck came into view headed north — the right direction.

The driver, an Australian, stopped and said, "Can I give you a lift, mate?"

"You sure can," I replied. "I'm headed for 80 Kilo. You see,

I'm too sick to work, and they have sent me back to the hospital camp."

The driver and his POW companion looked at me for a moment, then the driver's eyes drifted downward to my right leg.

"I see what you mean, mate," he replied as a wide grin spread slowly across his face. "You're in luck. That's just where we're going. We have to drop off a few bags of rice for the residents there." After a short pause, his grin vanished and he added, "Just don't expect too much when you get there, Yank."

The two Aussies climbed out of the truck cab and lifted me into the back of the vehicle where I lay across a couple of the rice bags. We took off in a cloud of dust for the twenty-kilometer ride, which took nearly two hours to complete. A million thoughts raced through my mind — *what was this so-called hospital I was headed for?* That Aussie's face and voice didn't seem to reflect much good news, I said aloud, as if talking over my situation. Things could be worse, I told myself. I'm really not that bad off. This is not going to get me down. I'm going to live through this — I *am* going to go back home after this is over.

Some two hours later, we pulled off the jungle highway through the unattended gate at 80 Kilo. I was wringing wet and physically exhausted from the day's ordeal. As we headed toward a nearby bamboo barracks, the Australians in the truck cab wrapped bandannas over their faces as a sharp, pungent odor swept over us like a bad dream. Two Dutch POWs, who turned out to be medical orderlies, made a litter with their hands and arms and lugged me into one of the long bamboo huts. Hundreds of men in varying stages of dying lay or sat in their small allotted spaces along the split bamboo platform as we passed through. We arrived at a cubicle about one hundred feet from the open end of the building, and the orderlies deposited me in an area that looked as if it already was full of sick men.

"Ve put you in American section," one of the Dutchmen said in broken English. They plodded off toward the end of the building, and my "hospital" companions made room for me in the middle of the section. There were thirty-five men already in this cubicle, including two of my American friends, Frank Faulkner and Harry Kitchings.

Back at the 100 Kilo work camp, death took the first member

of our officer corps shortly after my departure for the 80 Kilo
hospital. On July 31, 1943, Lt. R. W. Hampton died of complications from a severe attack of dysentery. Hampton was one of the
best-liked officers of the 2d Battalion. He was a tall, slender man
whose long strides reminded me of a farmer stepping off a wheat
field. His was a quiet, mild-mannered personality that permitted
him to get along splendidly with everyone, including the lowest
privates.

The following day things got even bleaker. Dr. Lumpkin, the
one man we looked to for medical succor, died of the same disease. In his desperate battle to save others, he couldn't even save
himself. The death of Dr. Lumpkin tore the very fibers of our
being, and our morale plummeted. If our own doctor was unable
to survive, could there be hope for any of us?

Eighty Kilo turned out to be my last official place of residence in that long struggle in the Burma jungles that had begun
nearly a year earlier at Moulmein. While the weeks and months
dragged on, and the dead and dying dominated the routine at
our sick camp, the railroad progressed toward completion deep
in the jungles.

The environment at the 80 Kilo sick camp defies description. The fact that Faulkner and Kitchings, both good friends
from Wichita Falls and from my own Headquarters Battery, were
present raised my spirits when I arrived there late in July. Both
these friends were about my own age, and Faulkner served with
me as a member of our battalion radio detail. However, both
men were seriously ill from severe ulcerations of the legs, and
neither was able to get up from his bed.

At any given time during our few months at 80 Kilo, several
hundred men lay there on the threshold of death, although the
actual count of those who passed through is known but to God.
The Japanese had told us that we no longer were of any use to
them, and that we had been sent there to die. Their words proved
prophetic; few of the patients survived.

Time at 80 Kilo was all but forgotten, and those four or five
months there became one continuous stagger on the brink of
death. This fantasy of dead and dying enveloped us in an infinite
realm of funereal sounds and smells. During the fourteen

months we were involved in building the Death Railway in Burma, 133 of our approximately 550 American POWs died. Of that total, forty-eight died at 80 Kilo Camp and fifty others at 100 Kilo. Our entire medical staff at the 80 Kilo Camp consisted of one Eurasian doctor — a member of the Dutch army — and two orderlies. The orderlies also helped with burial duties, as did a few other POWs who were able to get up off their backs. Often, so many lay dead that it took the burial party three days to remove a body from our sleeping area.

A few days following my transfer to 80 Kilo, our good friend Jimmy Alexander showed up with a severe tropical ulcer on his left leg. Jimmy also suffered from chronic dysentery. He was in pretty bad shape when they dumped him onto the platform near where I was wasting away. Back in 100 Kilo Camp when the work had become especially severe and most of us were moving about like zombies, tropical ulcers and other diseases began taking their toll, and more and more POWs joined the non-workers on the "desperately ill" roster. One day one of our group at 100 Kilo was dressing a big tropical ulcer on his leg. About the only treatment available was to flush the sores with hot water. Ironically, Jimmy had come up to this fellow, and apparently trying to cheer him up a bit, had said facetiously, "Gee, I wish I had one of those little old ulcers so I, too, could get out of work."

On September 26, 1943, Jimmy died of his ulcer and from complications brought on by dysentery. As he drew closer and closer to the end, I tried to talk him into clinging to life.

"Come on, Jimmy," I would plead. "You have so much to live for. We're going to get out of here soon and go home."

He would look at me with round, sunken eyes, and say nothing. His very silence was testimony to the extent of his misery and disease. He was virtually all skin and bones when he died. Dysentery had drained the very life from his body. He became too weak to sit up, and just before he died he lost control of his bowels. He had to use his canteen cup to catch the outflow. After his death, his body lay there three days before the burial party could take him on his final journey to the nearby graveyard.

Faulkner had preceded Jimmy in death, on September 8. His decline was agonizing, but by this time death was so common that the living had become somewhat immune to it. Faulkner had severe ulcers on both legs that extended into the feet. Some of his toes had dropped off. Several weeks before his death, he lost control of his mind, and several of us in the area took turns feeding him. The last week before he died, his mouth became infected, and some of his teeth fell out. On the morning of September 8, we awoke to find him dead. He was only twenty years old.

Kitchings, the only other American in my immediate area, hung on until October 14. Most of the other POWs in our section were British. Everybody there suffered from rotting tropical ulcers, and the stench must have been overwhelming. But when your own body is in the same state of decay as everyone else's, the smell goes unnoticed.

On the rare occasion that a Japanese guard walked through the area, he held a handkerchief over his nose and mouth, trying to filter out some of the smell. None ever lingered or showed any concern for our misfortunes.

Even now, fifty years after I watched Faulkner, Alexander, and Kitchings die, I still grieve. As it was when they died, it is a silent, inward grief. Jimmy Alexander was one of the brightest and funniest individuals I had ever been close to, even though he frequently put aside his intellect in his quest for a good time. Faulkner and Kitchings were barely past their teenage years. Neither ever experienced the bliss of marriage and children, the "bone of my bones, and flesh of my flesh" (Genesis 2:23). They never knew the joy of seeing a couple of bright grandchildren grow into adulthood.

They would never know that the cause for which they sacrificed their lives brought their nation to the pinnacle of international power and influence. Their GI buddies who returned helped create an unprecedented prosperity. Their contemporaries would fill the office of the President of the United States from the end of the war until 1993, and would dominate every branch of government. A Saudi Arabian general would say after the U.S.-led defeat of Saddam Hussein in 1991, "If the world is going to have only one superpower, thank God it is the United States of America." They did not die in vain.

Because I was at their side when these three friends died, I cite their passing in detail to show what was going on up and down the Burma-Thailand jungle railroad. Thousands of others went to eternity under similar circumstances — by its completion in October 1943, the railway had claimed 325 men for every mile of track. One became hardened to death, just put it back in the farthest recesses of the mind. Subconsciously, I became angry with death. This, in turn, made me more determined that I would live and see this ordeal through.

After having been hauled back to 80 Kilo, I began a routine of diligently nursing my ulcerated leg. Finally some of the black, dead flesh began to disappear around the edges and was replaced by a rim of baby pink, healing tissue. Sometime in early September, our Dutch doctor received a small quantity of iodoform, described in Webster's Dictionary as "a yellow, crystalline, volatile compound with a penetrating, persistent odor that is used as an antiseptic dressing." This golden substance was literally more valuable than gold. The doctor began dusting the iodoform on our ulcers with miraculous results.

An English lad housed in his "spacious" three-by-six-foot area just to my left soon became a close friend, since we had so much in common and nowhere to go. Each of us had ulcers on the mend, and our conversations began to toy with the idea that we just might survive our stay at 80 Kilo Camp. One morning the doctor, trailed by his two trusty orderlies, worked his way down the dusty aisle to view our ulcers and to contemplate our various other ills. As he approached my British buddy (sadly, I cannot recall his name), the Englishman slowly unwrapped the dirty, stained cloth from his ulcerated leg. To our utter surprise, his ulcer had gotten reinfected overnight, and once again was an angry, black mass of dead and dying flesh from his knee to the shin. The doctor just shook his head, frowned and moved on, motioning him to wrap the old rag back around his leg. The medical crew moved on to examine my own ulcer, and finding it still healing, sprinkled some of that precious golden dust on the sore. Two days later, my friend was dead.

Our bamboo huts were partitioned off, and we usually had between thirty-five and forty patients in each section. There were thirty-six men in the section, which became my world at 80 Kilo sick camp. Before I left a few months later, thirty-four of them were dead. The other survivor was an American who had his right leg amputated by an Australian surgeon who went from camp to camp in a Herculean effort to keep as many of the sick alive as possible.

Never during this period when I was flat on my back, fighting for life itself, nor over the entire forty-two-month ordeal as a POW, did I ever reach the point where I wanted to die, as so many did. Often we would spend hours trying to talk comrades out of dying. They would just give up — the will to live had deserted them. It became easier to die than to live. They knew they were going to die and had accepted the fact. It became easy to recognize a man who had accepted death — he was ready for it. A look of contentment would spread over his face, and he would just fade away. There was nothing you could do. Sometimes it took only an hour or two for the end to come; others would linger in this state for days. Often, I would make an effort to scold one of them, trying to shock him and rekindle a spark of the will to live. But when a guy was ready to die, he just died.

Sometimes, the death of a friend came in an atmosphere of unreal serenity. His buddy would sit beside him, often holding his hand, usually not saying a word. Life would depart peacefully, with the dying one knowing to the last that he was loved, and would be missed.

September, October, and November came and went with only the end of the monsoon marking their passage. I continued to heal, and soon I was able to get up off my pallet. I could hobble to a nearby ditch and use the "toilet." Once, when I became particularly hungry and had hardened my will to get out of that hell hole, I sent word through a POW truck driver to Maj. Winthrop Rodgers, my battery commander when I enlisted in the National Guard in 1938, that I needed some money to supplement our scant food rations. In a few days, the driver returned with ten dollars, and I was able to purchase a few blocks of dark sugar that helped sustain me. I will forever be grateful to "Windy" Rodgers for coming through for me.

Toward the end of 1943, I was well enough to rejoin my comrades still working on the railroad. I was trucked up to 114 Kilo Camp, the last of our working stations in Burma. By this time the railroad had been completed, and trains were passing through our area on a daily basis. I remained at 114 Kilo for several weeks, although I still was too weak to work. My ulcer remained a large, open wound, although it was mostly pink, growing flesh. It did not completely heal until after our release at the end of the war.

It was at 114 Kilo that I first came in contact with Dr. Henri H. Hekking, a marvelous Dutch physician who grew up in the Netherlands East Indies, and who practiced medicine there. Dr. Hekking had been treating many of our American POWs, and thanks to his unusual abilities, few under his charge died. Many of our group credited Dr. Hekking with having saved their lives.

I had a smaller ulcer on my left leg, and while it never went wild and spread across the entire leg, nonetheless it had existed in a state of blackness for months. Upon arrival at 114 Kilo, I became a patient of Dr. Hekking, and that black ulcer finally met its match. Dr. Hekking's method of treatment was to literally scrape dead flesh from ulcerated areas with the sharp edge of a silver dessert spoon. There was no anesthetic, so when the good doctor arrived to "treat" an ulcer, he was accompanied by two to four orderlies who substituted brute strength for anesthetic. The orderlies grabbed the patient's arms and legs and held on grimly while the doctor scraped out the dead flesh. The method worked, but it was a most painful procedure. The patient would wad up a corner of his blanket, stuff it between his teeth, and bite down as hard as possible to help him endure the excruciating pain.

Early in 1943, Group Three, which included about two hundred of our 2d Battalion and USS *Houston* survivors, had arrived in Burma for railroad duty without any medical personnel. The Japanese assigned Dr. Hekking to this group, but many of its survivors insist he also was sent by God.

The Dutch physician immediately took a liking to the Americans, and they became lifelong friends. His methods of treatment went far beyond those of a regular medical doctor. Later, Otto Schwarz, a *Houston* veteran, said he had "always marveled at the record that our group had in the Burma jungles."

"We only lost thirteen men all the time Doc Hekking was with us," Schwarz said. "He also did not perform a single amputation. All this while in the other camps, men were dying at a much higher rate, and many amputations were being performed."

Schwarz said for years that he had attributed Dr. Hekking's success to his knowledge of jungle and tropical diseases gained from years spent in thhe region. But Schwarz came to the conclusion years later that it was something far beyond medical knowledge. He and others close to the good doctor are convinced Dr. Hekking "had special powers unknown to us."

Numerous survivors of the Burma death camp insist that Dr. Hekking became known for his "presence." Usually, when visiting a patient deep in the jungles, he would sit beside the soldier and engage him in conversation. Then, he would touch the patient, placing his hand on the man's brow, and the man would feel better.

With the completion of the railroad, the Japs soon began shipping the Burma contingent out of the jungle to camps in Thailand where they had established several permanent POW compounds. One day early in 1944, several dozen of us were loaded onto empty boxcars and hauled out on the very railroad that so many of our comrades had died while building. It was a glorious day to escape that abominable jungle. I had survived, despite the fact that when I was shunted back to the 80 Kilo sick camp, none of my friends had expected to see me alive again.

But I had made it! After several hours on that bumpy, dangerous railroad, we arrived at Camp 2, Kanburi, where we stayed only a few weeks. We then were moved to nearby Tamarkan, a huge POW compound near the Kwae Noi River, also known as the River Kwai — made famous by the British book that became a movie entitled, *Bridge Over the River Kwai*. The year I spent at Tamarkan, located near the Thai town of Kanchanaburi, would produce most of the fond memories I retain of my forty-two months as a prisoner of war.

10.

The Good Days

AFTER THAT INTERMINABLE year in the Burma jungle, Tamarkan was a welcome relief, a comparative heaven on earth. It housed several thousand prisoners and was situated on an open area less than one hundred yards from the north bank of the Kwae Noi. It was miles out of the jungle — which was good, but a major steel bridge crossing the river was situated only yards away from a corner of the compound — which was bad; the bridge was a natural target for Allied bombers. To make matters worse, the Japanese brought in a battery of antiaircraft guns and placed them between the POW compound and the railway tracks to protect the target from the predictable bombing.

Our rations improved since we had returned to an area that was inhabited by other humans. Transporting the food to our camp was no problem; the area was served not only by a major rail line, but roads that were actually paved and saw regular traffic.

As soon as the railroad was connected in the jungles, the Japanese faced the mammoth task of trying to figure out what to do with the tens of thousands of POWs that had been congregated in Thailand. Some were shuttled back to the Changi jail in Singapore. Others — those who were physically able — were dispatched eastward toward Saigon, French Indochina, en route to the Japanese mainland. Hundreds eventually would drown when Allied submarines blasted the Japanese ships hauling them out of the water. Among those who perished at sea in this manner were eighteen of our army and navy comrades.

For several weeks after arriving at Tamarkan, I remained on the sick list of those still recuperating from jungle illnesses. I was excused from details, although only a few hundred POWs were sent out of camp daily on labor details. Our captors had agreed to the construction of a theater in the middle of the parade ground at Tamarkan, and soon I began hanging out there on a regular basis. I struck up a friendship with an Australian and an Englishman, Frank Brydges of Sydney, and John Branchflower of Manchester, England. We soon became close buddies, especially John and I. Frank was an illustrator with the Sydney *Herald,* and John worked in a factory in Manchester.

John was only about five feet, four inches tall, and since I was over eight inches taller, we must have looked like Mutt and Jeff of the Depression-era comic pages. John was a couple of years my senior, was married, and had two young daughters. He had pictures of his wife and children, and we spent hours in conversation about family life back in England. John had a keen sense of humor and often played comedy roles in our theater productions.

Branchflower had already seen a lot of war when I met him in early 1944. But his disposition was typically British — he faced his destiny with outward unconcern. He always looked at the brighter side of an issue, and inevitably succeeded in cheering me up when my moods were down. He had a somewhat broad nose below brown eyes that twinkled in merriment. His wide smile was infectious, and he generally kept Brydges and me in a cheerful mood.

Branchflower had a browntone picture of himself with his wife, Leah, and their first daughter, Pauline, who was about a year old when it was made. Before we parted after the war, he gave the picture to me as a remembrance. He had carried it with him through several battles against the Germans in North Africa and later against the Japanese in Malaya and Singapore.

At one period, apparently after his capture in Singapore, he wrote on the back of the picture, "never heard from Leah for 7 months now, don't know whether our new baby is a girl or boy."

Later, he learned the second child was another daughter. On still another area of the back side of the picture, he wrote, "We have been prisoners over 2 years; be glad when we are going home again. Many falling down with dysentery. Wondering & hoping that Leah & Pauline & our new baby are o.k."

Frank Brydges was about six years older than Branchflower, and was the father figure of our little trio. Frank, being an artist, was in charge of creating costumes and scenery backgrounds for our theater. I soon joined the "Theater Party" as Frank's assistant.

We produced full-blown Broadway shows about every fortnight. The Theater Party included an orchestra made up of remnants of the Royal Army band whose members had somehow managed to hang onto their instruments after two years of captivity. Most of the actors were British, although there were a few Dutch and Australians in the cast. Once Frank talked me into acting in a small skit, but it turned out so bad that I stuck with my stagehand chores thereafter.

Most of the costumes were made of gunny sacks that came into the camp full of rice. We used split bamboo matting to create background scenery. Soot mixed with water became black paint. White lime and curry powder were the ingredients for other colors. We would mix the three substances to get various hues; some of the work turned out to be pretty realistic, thanks to Frank's artistic abilities.

Compared to what we had just endured in Burma, the time in Tamarkan proved a pleasant respite. The Japanese had modulated their behavior, although they still bashed people about for minor infractions. This was their way of life, and they were unable, or unwilling to change. Our theater group, however, was left pretty much on its own since the guards rarely came inside our compound.

Everybody who could walk turned up for our productions. Even the Japanese came, and naturally, they occupied the choice front-row sitting area. There were no chairs, so everybody would sit on the ground during the performances. The Japanese seemed to thoroughly enjoy the shows, although most of them could understand little of the dialogue.

On the Emperor's birthday, in the early months of 1944, the Japanese declared a holiday and gave us extra rations. Following what would have been an unimaginably sumptuous lunch back in the jungle, our captors decided to challenge the American POWs to a baseball game. Our group was somewhat reluctant to get involved, but when the Japanese issued a challenge, acceptance was automatic — to refuse would have brought their wrath down on our heads.

After laying out the diamond, the Japanese sergeant asked, "Who umpire?" Nobody moved a muscle. Again, in a sterner voice, the sergeant asked, "Who umpire?" Still no response. It was obvious he would soon lose his cool, so I reluctantly moved up a couple of steps and "volunteered" to serve as umpire.

My legs were wobbly and my disbelieving brain shouted, What are you doing here, dummy! as I stepped behind home plate. The game was fairly routine for an inning or two; then, as a Japanese guard stepped up to the plate, our pitcher appeared to have gotten a second wind and began hurling the ball with impressive speed and accuracy. The Jap swung and missed, then hit a foul for his second strike. I held my breath as the third ball whizzed toward the plate. The guard just stood there, and I weakly hissed, "Strike three!" This fellow, who literally had the power of life or death over me, whirled and began gesticulating wildly and jabbering away in Japanese. His brown face became a darker brown as he bulldozed me backward with his chest. I thought I had had it, but fortunately, the Japanese sergeant intervened. I have no idea what he told the guard but he must have said that when the ump calls a batter out, he's out. I don't remember who won, or even when the game ended. I did determine, however, that this would be the end of my umpiring career.

The monsoon having ended well before we were shipped out of the jungles, the sky remained a deep blue and a warm sun kept everything blissfully dry during the early months I spent at Tamarkan. The British and Australians had exempted their members of the Theater Party from outside work duty, and I had thought the same rule applied to me. But alas, it didn't, and since I had almost fully recovered from the worst of my jungle illnesses, trouble soon found me.

I had no close American buddies left at Tamarkan, although there were a hundred or so of us in the camp at the time. Some of my best friends had died back in the jungles, and others, including my old latrine-digging buddy Dub Reed, had been shipped out to Saigon or back to Singapore. First Lieutenant Eldon Schmid of Service Battery was the ranking American officer in Tamarkan.

Early in 1944 the Allies had gained control of the air over the whole of this region, and bombing runs were on the increase by the time I arrived at Tamarkan. Most of these raids during the earlier period were on and around Bangkok, or other more prominent targets around the countryside. As soon as we had completed the Thailand-Burma railroad, the Japanese began running trains at frequent intervals toward northern Burma, where they were bogged down in a bitter struggle with British and American forces attacking from India.

Allied bombing raids came more frequently, and soon they began working over our railroad. This, in turn, led to the need for additional work groups to repair damage back in the jungle. Soon, my name turned up on one of those lists.

A work party going back to the jungle included about one hundred men. When our captors called for a jungle work crew, it was formed proportionally from among the British, Dutch, Australians, and Americans. Since we Yanks were such a small segment of the camp, usually there were only one or two of us assigned to the group heading back into that diabolic forest.

The news that I was on the list of those headed back into Burma left me totally shattered. To begin with, I felt it unfair that Americans did not receive exemption from outside work as did other nationalities assigned to the Theater Party, but my plea fell on Schmid's deaf ear.

"You're going back, and that's it," Schmid told me. I felt he was picking on me because I was not a member of his Lubbock Service Battery group.

I began to pack my few personal items for travel, then went over to the theater area to tell Frank and John what had happened to me.

"I know for sure I never will come back alive," I told Frank. "There's just no way I can take another stint in that hell hole."

"Well, mate," Frank mused, "let's just see what we can do."

He went out and was gone for about ten minutes. Meantime, Branchflower tried to console me, but nothing he said eased my anxiety.

Soon Frank returned and said to me, "Go to your bed. Your temperature is 105 degrees and you're very sick."

"I am? Do you think we can get by with this?" I asked.

"No problem, mate," Frank replied. "I have a cobber who is the chief medical orderly over at the hospital. He'll square it with your lieutenant. Don't you worry one bit."

I hurried to my pallet and wrapped my blanket tightly about my body. I was trying to work up a sweat, and even raise my temperature a bit if possible.

It took only ten minutes for Lieutenant Schmid, followed by his brother, Ellis, a sergeant also in Service Battery, to reach my bedside.

"There's absolutely nothing wrong with you," the lieutenant bellowed. "Here, let me take your temperature." He shoved a thermometer toward my mouth.

"I think my fever may have broken by now," I said meekly, trying my best to sound like a recovering malaria patient.

"You're not sick!" Schmid insisted. He shoved the thermometer under my tongue, and waited impatiently for it to register.

Sure enough, my temperature was about normal.

"See, I told you!" he shouted. "We'll just see about this."

The two Schmids stalked out, and I crawled deeper under my blanket.

Technically, there was nothing Schmid could do in my case. I had been officially placed on the sick list by Frank's medical friend, and the work party departed later that day without me. I never knew who was assigned to my place on the work crew, but I was determined not to go back to the land of the dead.

I didn't let Lieutenant Schmid's wrath upset me too much because, frankly, I just plain disliked the fellow. Schmid was somewhat typical of well over half our battalion's officers — they just didn't amount to much. Most of them had received their commissions during the peacetime years before World War II, and that little bar on their shoulders made them think they really were officers and gentlemen. I did not know many, if any, of my contemporaries — with the possible exception of his brother, Ellis — who ever became close friends with Schmid. Perhaps that's a bit harsh on the fellow, but at any rate, I have no regrets at having outsmarted him in this instance.

I am convinced Frank saved my life. I knew intuitively that I would not survive another tour in the jungle.

Frank came over to my bunk later and said, "How are you feeling, mate?"

"I'm feeling a lot better, but I'm afraid that Lieutenant Schmid will get me for this," I replied.

"Never you mind," Frank said. "We've got it all fixed. You are a member of the Theater Party, and that subject is now closed."

And it was, until all of us were shipped out to other camps toward the end of 1944.

Meanwhile, Allied bombers began dropping their loads of destruction in our vicinity, and soon they began working over the steel bridge spanning the river near the corner of our compound. Being in the vicinity of falling and exploding bombs was as terrifying at Tamarkan as it had been at Camp Singasari or on the *Dai Moji Maru*. The Japs refused to allow us to dig trenches inside our camp, but there was a drainage ditch crossing the area where most of us huddled during these raids.

The Allied bombers initially struck our railroad bridge as a secondary target. Usually one or two bombers would make a pass at it and move on out of the area. Prisoner of war laborers had constructed a wooden bridge across the river several hundred feet downstream from the steel structure, and this temporary bridge was destroyed on the first bombing raid in the area.

During these raids, we huddled in our drainage ditch, and I closed my eyes tightly and covered my head with my hands, somehow feeling this would shield me. After surviving a few of these raids, one day I got up enough courage to watch the bombers as they made their run toward our bridge.

The raiders appeared to be four or five thousand feet up, and I watched, fascinated, as the bomb bay doors opened and those little sticks seemed to shoot out its rear end. They arched slowly and then began descending straight down toward my nose. I said to myself, This is it! They're going to hit right where I'm lying. But they didn't, and I heard the explosions seconds later in the vicinity of the bridge.

Since the bombs had missed me on that occasion, the next raid saw my courage grow a bit. I continued to watch as the next cluster descended faster and faster toward me. At a height of what seemed to be only a hundred feet above me, the bombs appeared to curve away and blasted the bridge area again. Later I was told by one of my British friends, who had been at war two years before America became involved, that this was the route bombs always seem to take if they were falling anywhere in your vicinity.

Once two B-24s began zeroing in on our bridge in a low-level bombing raid. The first one swooped right over the middle of our camp and dropped four bombs at the structure. As the second followed right on his tail, seemingly only a few hundred feet over our heads, Branchflower punched me in the ribs, and I nearly jumped out of our ditch.

"I can see a bit of paper that came out of his bomb bay," Branchflower whispered in my ear. "Let's see what it is."

The bit of paper had settled on the ground a few feet away. John crawled over and picked it up.

"Blimey!" he exclaimed. "It's a bloody chewing gum wrapper."

We looked at it in awe. It was a Wrigley's Spearmint gum wrapper, and it even still smelled like gum. Our mouths began salivating, and after a moment we shook our fists toward the departing bomber.

"Why didn't you leave the gum in it, you bastard?" Branchflower yelled softly. We looked at each other, then began laughing. It broke the tension of being under aerial siege.

Moments prior to one of these raids, Branchflower and I had been working on some scenery at the theater when the alert sounded. We could hear the sirens from nearby Kanchanaburi, and we scurried out the back and flung ourselves in the nearby drainage ditch. This raid was heavier than normal, and bomber after bomber swept over the area. Bombs were exploding all about, although none actually fell inside our camp. Branchflower and I reached a state of panic simultaneously. We looked at each other, and without a word, jumped to our feet and dashed madly across the compound to another area of our ditch. We were fortunate that none of the Japanese guards were watching at the time or we may have been shot; we were under strict orders not to show ourselves during a bombing raid.

Neither of us could explain why we suddenly got up and exposed ourselves to extreme danger to seek what must have seemed at the time a safer place to hug the earth. Panic, of course, is often hard to control, and this was one of those times. The middle of my back always twinged during bombing raids, as if that point of my anatomy was the bull's eye for the falling bombs. I just knew that if I remained in that place another second a bomb would fall right between my shoulder blades. Branchflower said he had an identical feeling, so we fled to "safety."

As the bombing runs increased in the area, the Japanese antiaircraft squad guarding the nearby river bridge got fresh reinforcements. This battery of guns was just outside our compound fence. For weeks it had been blasting away at Allied aircraft passing over the area en route to targets in the Bangkok vicinity.

I came down with a severe attack of malaria and was moved from my hut, which was adjacent to the fence where the antiaircraft guns were situated, across the compound to the hospital. On the very day I moved, the Allies decided to do something about our pesky antiaircraft guns, although none of us ever witnessed these weapons shoot down any of the raiders.

It was just about 5:00 P.M. and all outside workers had returned to camp. Everybody able to stand congregated on the parade ground in front of the theater for the daily Japanese *tinko*. Since I had moved to the hospital hut, I was exempt from this formation. The Japanese were meticulous about keeping up with every POW in their charge. Even during the darkest days of heavy work back in the jungles, the daily *tinkos* were held without fail. We would line up by nationality and there would be hell to pay if a single person was missing. Often, it would take half a dozen or more nose counts before our overlords were satisfied.

Just as the assembled POWs had settled into their formations, a distant rumble to the west could be heard, barely audible at first, then growing in intensity. Everyone instantly recognized what it was — a formation of about two dozen Allied bombers headed directly for our camp. The formation was only a few thousand feet in the air, and had slipped into our vicinity virtually unnoticed. Their destination proved to be the nearby antiaircraft guns.

As the bombers approached, the Japanese guards bolted for their trenches near their quarters, and the assembled POWs scattered in every direction. The antiaircraft guns began blasting away at the incoming raiders. The bombers never wavered; they flew right at us, keeping a perfect formation. The tactic used on the battery of guns is known as blanket bombing. The formation let go all at once, and bomb after bomb fell earthward. One by one, the antiaircraft guns were silenced as the explosives saturated the area. Unfortunately, a dozen or more of the big firecrackers strayed across the POW compound fence, blasting a few of our flimsy huts into a million bamboo toothpicks.

Fourteen POWs, mostly Australians, were killed. After the dust settled, I went to the area where the bombs had invaded our compound to inspect the damage. A large crater gaped right where I had been staying before moving across camp to the hospital. I felt that perhaps the severity of my malaria attack was an act of God, or I might have been right where that bomb hit.

The steel railroad bridge near our camp at Tamarkan had an interesting history. It originally spanned a river in Java. The Japanese disassembled the structure there, packed it in large crates, and shipped it to Thailand where it was reassembled to cross the Kwae Noi near our camp. The bridge is still in use today, although its middle spans had to be rebuilt following continuous bombing raids throughout 1944.

The transshipment of this bridge is typical of what the Japanese did in countries they occupied across Southeast Asia. They systematically stripped strategic materials from dozens of conquered nations and shipped most back to Japan for use in the war effort. The region is rich in resources such as rubber, oil, tin, and other metals which were in short supply in Japan itself. It must have taken years for some of these Asian countries to recover from the rape of their natural resources.

After we buried the dead from that raid, things settled down again and our Theater Party got back into its routine. By this time an Australian named Les Luff, a survivor of the *Perth,* whose home is in Maffra, Victoria, had joined our little trio of prop-and-scenery crew. (Forty-five years after the end of World War II, Luff and I would reestablish contact, and he and his wife would come to Texas as our guests. I was serving as the 1991 president of the Lost Battalion Association, and our annual reunion met that year in Austin. Luff and his wife Doris spent two weeks at our home, and there were ample opportunities to rehash the "good old POW days.")

The latter half of 1944 found me and my international circle of friends in reasonably good health and, considering the circumstances, leading a somewhat peaceful existence. The monsoon had resumed its relentless inundation of everything in its path. While the downpours did not seem to bother us as they had back in the jungles, on one occasion, they performed an astonishing feat straight from the pages of *Ripley's Believe It or Not.* After one particularly energetic deluge had abated, we went outside to find little fish swimming about in shallow pools on our parade ground. The area of our camp was on a knoll, and it is inconceivable that they could have swum from a pool or stream up to our parade ground. The unhappy creatures must have been sucked up with the moist air over the sea and deposited, appropriately, in our prison compound.

Our Theater Party boasted a cast of quite talented individuals. The staff consisted of musicians, composers, actors, writers, and, of course, our accomplished quartet of costume and scenery designers. Frank Brydges, who made our little group really click, had a mild, friendly approach and enormous creative ability. His sets and scenery conveyed a realism that not only empowered the actors, but held the audiences in their spell and then released them, homesick from their brief visit "home."

Those responsible for putting together these shows always were on the lookout for new music. Once, I volunteered to help one of our musicians reduce the song "I Don't Want to Set The World on Fire," to paper so the band could use it in a musical.

After several attempts, we gave up. That was the end of my not-too-promising musical career.

One song composed by a member of our group, whose name I cannot remember, turned into an instant hit — a melody filled with memories, one that worked its way hauntingly into the minds of so many of us. Years later, I found and visited Frank Brydges while on a trip to Australia. We pieced together the lyrics with growing enthusiasm until we had completely recalled "At the End of the Day"

> At the end of the day,
> Some soft music I play
> And I let my heart go free.
> For the day had been hard and long,
> Only with song could I bring you to me.
> In the evening at last as hours passed,
> The jungle lay quite still.
> I sing to my love as the moon up above
> Goes slowly over the hill.
> A faint touch of breeze
> That just rustles the trees
> As it swept and swayed the air,
> And I think of our loved ones fair,
> So very dear to everyone there.
> In the twilight I live anew
> The things we used to do.
> One day we'll be free,
> Oh what heaven for you and me!

This little tune was an instant success; it expressed closely the state of mind of so many of us throughout those months in the jungles. It was introduced in one of our productions by a British POW from London named P. H. Fox, who not only had a good voice, but became our leading actor. Fox was a tall, slim fellow with a prominent hooked nose. He would move across the stage, or, when not acting, around the parade ground with a long, bobbing stride that reminded one of a camel crossing the desert. He was very popular and soon became a celebrity in camp.

Two other actors stood out in our group. One was another English chap named David, a handsome bloke who often played leading male roles. The other was a Dutch army Eurasian, who had delicate features and developed into a sensational female impersonator. This fellow had dark brown eyes with long, curling eyelashes, and a smooth olive complexion. He was five feet, five inches tall and weighed about 130 pounds — the perfect size for a female impersonator — and when he was made up with a wig and what served as cosmetics, he was a dead ringer for the real thing.

John Branchflower was no slouch on the stage himself. His diminutive stature, combined with his natural comic ability, made him a popular regular in most of our productions. Branchflower was identical in size to John G. Tower, United States senator from Texas from 1961 to 1985, whom I served as press secretary for three years in the 1970s.

Fox and the female impersonator became good friends and often played opposite each other in male-female roles. Inevitably, rumors began circulating that they might be more than just fellow actors. The female impersonator quickly became a celebrity, but not of the sort he sought. Some of the guys around camp began issuing flirtatious whistles and catcalls as he walked about. Shortly, this all became too humiliating and he quit the stage. The loss of our best female impersonator deprived the Theater Party of one of its best actors. He told us one night after an unusually good performance that it was his last, as he could not continue being confined in close quarters with thousands of POWs who had not been in the company of actual females for nearly three years.

There never was the least bit of evidence that this fellow had any homosexual tendencies — to my knowledge no homosexual problems of any sort ever surfaced during our forty-two months as prisoners. It is of course possible that homosexual activities existed, but it was conducted in secret — these were days far before the emergence of the relative tolerance we now see in American society.

Sex tends to be a dominant topic of conversation around a group of military men. Our armed forces in World War II were made up almost exclusively of men; women served in separate, (strictly supportive) units. There was no gender mixing in the military until long after the end of the Second World War.

Therefore, it should not be surprising that sex remained in our conversations and thoughts for the first few months of captivity. But as our POW experience dragged on, we began giving sex and food about equal attention. As food got scarcer and our bodies began deteriorating from hunger and disease, it shoved aside all else to dominate our thoughts, meditations, and even our dreams. While, as the Bible states, "man cannot live by bread alone," we quickly learned that he cannot live at all without it.

With our harrowing jungle experience behind us, our health improved somewhat at Tamarkan. With it, our interest in the future improved as well. As our friendship developed, John Branchflower and I frequently talked about what it was like to be married. Naturally, the sex life of husband and wife came up occasionally, and since I was only nineteen and single when captured, I urged John to talk about his own encounter with marriage.

"Aye, lad, it's heaven itself," Branchflower would muse, a sly grin broadening his face.

"What's it like to be a father?" I once asked him.

"Wonderful," he replied. "My two bonny lasses are something special." He pulled out the picture of his wife and eldest child and showed them to me again.

"I'll admit I wanted a boy each time my wife got in the family way," Branchflower disclosed during one of our talks. "Once I accused her of clipping them off and tucking it in so they would be girls," he said, laughing heartily.

With the POW compound at Tamarkan close to the river, water was never as scarce as it was back in the jungles. About once a week during the dry season our guardians allowed us to bathe in the river. Somebody was forever talking about how many species of flesh-eating fish existed in Thailand. Although I suspected such "experts" had about the same virtually nonexistant knowledge of aquatic life in the tropics as I did, I nonetheless kept a sharp eye out for anything carnivorous in the water during these bathing excursions. Our baths ceased during the monsoon, as the river's size swelled a hundredfold from the continuous downpours. So, instead of bathing in the river, one could simply stand in the downpour for a shower.

Around mid-1944 the Japanese told us that President Roosevelt had died, and someone named Truman had succeeded him. None of us had ever heard of Truman, but our captors appeared to enjoy telling us of Roosevelt's death. They had looked on him as their number one enemy. Nippon seemed to take the death of FDR as a good omen, not realizing that the gutsy Harry S. Truman would make the decision to drop the atom bombs that ended the war.

Late in 1944 we received our very first issue of American Red Cross packages. There were not enough to give one to each POW, so we shared one box among two or three prisoners. Although the quantity was not substantial, just to touch, just to smell bits of real food and real American cigarettes was to touch heaven itself. The boxes held tinned meats, hardtack biscuits, a variety of cheeses, and a few other treasures, in addition to the smokes.

During the night after the Red Cross food was distributed, I was awakened by a swarm of large rats whose keen noses had picked up the smell of real cheese. They were determined to have it. We had a difference of opinion, and after fighting them off, I wrapped my precious food in some pieces of rag and slept with my head on the bundle the rest of the night. The Red Cross provisions supplemented our usual cup of rice and watery stew for several days.

It became generally known that the Japanese army confiscated most of the Red Cross food supplies sent to our area for Allied prisoners. On several occasions Japanese soldiers were seen marching in formation past POW camps with American Red Cross packages strapped to their backpacks. Perhaps they are not to be judged too harshly — food and supplies became scarce late in the war when Allied bombers made it virtually impossible to move anything either by land or sea.

At about the same time the Red Cross packages arrived, we received our first shipment of mail from home. I got three short letters written on folded sheets apparently furnished by the Red Cross. They had been written by my father over a period of several weeks and contained general information about our family. It was obvious that he had been instructed to say nothing that would cause the Japanese censors to destroy the communication. The letters conjured up memories of our house, of home, of him. I thought, as I hadn't in a long while, of my last week before I left for the army. My father had worked my tail off in a carpentry project. We had sweated and laughed and pulled together. I thought about my mother, the center of my love of home. I thought about the old life that we had.

On a very few occasions, some of us actually had compassion for the plight of the Japanese soldier — the fighting soldiers, as opposed to our guards, who merited no such consideration. One such occasion came on a dreary day deep in the Burma jungles while the monsoon was at its peak and the Death Railway was months away from completion. We were out on one of those interminable railroad jobs when, at about midday, Japanese soldiers materialized from nowhere and began filtering through our area. These were front-line fighting men, carrying all their personal gear, weapons, and ammunition. Some were pulling small artillery pieces and mortars. They were headed for battle.

These hapless enemy soldiers were at the end of their ropes. They were literally on the verge of starvation and had all but exhausted their energy. We learned that each had been issued a couple of pounds of rice on the Thailand edge of the jungles, and told to report for duty in Burma where transportation was available. This was a forced march of over two hundred miles. They were needed as reinforcements in northern Burma where their army was bogged down in heavy fighting with Allied forces.

We had taken a short break to have lunch. The enemy soldiers were so pitiful that we shared our meager rice and soup rations with them. Most of them had no drinkable water, so we gave them something to drink, too. There was no sacrifice in that; water was never short in the jungles of Burma, just dangerous: drinking it without purification led inevitably to serious illness or death. We always boiled water at least fifteen minutes before considering it potable.

These troops were probably the friendliest of any enemy soldiers we came in contact with during our captivity. After expressing their profound thanks to us, they passed on through our work area and disappeared from our lives. None of us ever dwelt on the thought that we were assisting enemy soldiers. We looked on them as fellow sufferers in dire need in the midst of a hostile jungle. What else could we do?

Later, after the railroad was completed, we saw train after train loaded with troops pass our camp at Tamarkan, headed north, presumably for the Burma front. Southbound trains were usually either empty or carried wounded soldiers back to hospitals in the Bangkok area. The Japanese, as part of their Shinto religion, place a great deal of emphasis on the worship of ancestors. The dictionary describes Shintoism as "the indigenous religious cult of Japan consisting chiefly in the reverence of the spirits of natural forces, emperors, and heroes." Whenever an empty train passed us headed north on our railroad, some wag would comment, "There goes another load of ancestors up to the front to help the Jap troops."

Christmas, 1944 — our third in captivity — was a momentous occasion. Camp leaders began planning for it weeks in advance. We pooled our funds and bought as much extra rice and vegetables as the Japanese permitted. Church of England chaplains conducted special religious services for which virtually the entire compound turned out. Dinner followed these services, and there was enough food for everybody. We even had a somewhat generous ration of rice pudding for dessert. What a luxurious sensation it was to have a belly full of food. Fifty years later I still can recall the ebullience of actually having enough food to feel stuffed!

As 1944 ended, the Japanese command began implementing new plans, which we later learned were designed to defend the area against an Allied invasion. We began to notice subtle changes among our enemy. The whole atmosphere had a different feeling. All the guards who had been with us in the jungles were replaced with new personnel. Our new wardens had less and less contact with their soldiers or us, and they rarely showed up inside our compound. We felt hope, but it was a hope tempered by mounting despair as disease and labor cut an ever-widening swath through our numbers.

Shortly after the beginning of the new year, our officers and enlisted men were separated and placed in different compounds. It was obvious that, should there be an Allied invasion in the area, the Japanese did not want hordes of prisoners left with officers in charge to organize an uprising in the rear while their troops were off repelling the invaders.

11.

The Thousandth Cup

IN JANUARY 1945, POWs at Tamarkan began moving out daily to new compounds located along a crescent some ninety miles from Bangkok. Prisoners in these camps were put to work building emergency airfields, gun emplacements, and other types of fortifications to be used in defense against an invasion. These ramparts were strung along a line of approximately one hundred miles between Bangkok and the Indian Ocean, the most likely route for an invasion force.

We once again boarded the evil little Asian boxcars and moved through Bangkok. It was a dreadful time to go through that city as it was visited daily by Allied bombers. Our group paused only briefly there to transfer from the train to trucks, and we breathed a sigh of relief as we left the city and entered the open countryside. Our destination turned out to be the Camp 9, Phet Buri POW compound, situated almost in the shadow of a small, lonely mountain about ninety kilometers from Bangkok.

Frank Brydges and John Branchflower, my two best friends of Theater Party fame, stayed behind at Tamarkan. I would be reunited with Branchflower in another camp in the last few weeks of captivity, but would not see Brydges again until our Australian reunion thirty-six years after the war.

I did, however, gain a new friend at Phet Buri, a Scotsman named G. M. "Jock" McKenney. As Branchflower and I had, we became instant friends. Jock's home was in Bearsden, Glasgow, Scotland. Before leaving Phet Buri, we exchanged addresses and promised to keep in touch after the war ended. Of my British and Australian friends, Jock was the only one who corresponded with me after we returned home. In one of his first letters, he enclosed a foot-square piece of green silk which he had cut from a parachute used to drop supplies to POWs still remaining there. We had left by then; Americans were the first to be repatriated.

McKenney was a most friendly fellow. He spoke in a charming Scottish accent, and his friendship at Phet Buri filled the void left when I was shipped out of Tamarkan, leaving Frank Brydges and John Branchflower behind.

I stumbled into a bit of luck at Phet Buri. I still had the remnants of tropical ulcers on both legs and managed to evade most of the working parties that went outside the camp daily. One day our guardians asked for the services of anyone who had experience in carpentry. I stepped forward since I had served briefly as a carpenter's helper to my father back in Wichita Falls. This, I concluded, was enough experience to fulfill whatever needs the Japanese had, and also would serve to keep me off those work parties.

It turned into quite a break. The work was moderately light, and not too demanding of my modest skills. I also had opportunities to snitch a few extra crumbs of food left about by the guards. Most of my duties consisted of minor repairs to some crude buildings and articles such as wooden benches and tables used in the Japanese section of the camp.

At about this time, I witnessed the torture of Thai men arrested as suspected saboteurs. Usually the guards would shoo me away from the area, but a few times they ignored my presence as they questioned a suspect. On one such occasion the Thai was tied to a wooden bench and warm water was forced down his throat. After having to ingest an inordinate amount of this liquid, the subject then received heavy blows with a club on his stomach to force him to reveal whatever his torturers sought.

I sat quietly in a corner, trying to remain as inconspicuous as possible. Reputedly, this torture causes excruciating pain in the intestines; from the reaction of the victims, it succeeded. I saw at other times sharp bamboo slivers driven under finger- and toenails. I was never privy to the end results of these sessions; the victims usually were dragged or carried to other areas never to be seen again. There were reports that the Japanese usually ended up executing the Thais arrested in roundups of suspected saboteurs.

My sojourn as a carpenter lasted for about a month. During this brief interlude, I came across a valuable piece of information which subsequently led to a tasty repast. The Japanese sergeant who was second in command at Phet Buri had a pen of chickens from which he enjoyed fresh eggs every day. Since I was working in the area, I carefully studied the terrain around the pen and stored the details for future action.

The short period as camp carpenter meant an easy time for me and it passed too quickly. I was never comfortable while in close contact with the Japanese, even while they treated me somewhat kindly, as they did here. Most of my work consisted of simple repairs to crude furniture and other such types of light carpentry. Once I was asked to build some bookshelves in one of the buildings, and my heart leapt into my throat in the fear that my skill was not sufficient for the task. But it turned out fairly well, although it would not have won any awards for its workmanship.

Having completed the carpentry chores assigned by our captors, I was sent back to the regular ranks. My mind was still on those succulent hens in the Jap sergeant's pen, and my first thought was to design a plan to filch one. Dempsey Key immediately came to mind — the pair of us had successfully stolen the stalk of bananas outside a British officer's hut back in Camp Changi. I shared my strategic hen pen information with Key, and we immediately began formulating a plan of action.

The monsoons of 1945 had not yet arrived, so we did not have the cover of a dark, dreary, rainy night. We waited a few days until there was no moon, and then, about two hours after the sun went down, we launched Operation Hen Pen.

Dempsey Key turned out to be an excellent chicken thief. Under our plan, the two of us slowly crawled on our stomachs until we reached the back of the fence that contained our prey. I helped Key pull the fence up enough for him to slither underneath, then remained on watch as he proceeded to the hen roost. It seemed that he took an inordinate amount of time to return, but it was actually less than two minutes. He had his right hand around the neck of a limp chicken, and we scurried back on our bellies to a safe distance, then got up and ran triumphantly to our barracks.

The Japanese had become somewhat lax in overseeing our minute-by-minute activities. Often a dozen or more small cooking fires burned just outside our hut. Key and I hurriedly plucked the feathers from our prized hen. I took this incriminating evidence and dumped it into a nearby deep ditch we used as our latrine. When I returned, Key had come up with a tin gallon bucket, and already was boiling our chicken. In about half an hour we judged it to be sufficiently cooked, took the booty inside our hut, and devoured it. After having dumped the cleaned bones in the same repository as the feathers, we sacked out just in time for the 10:00 P.M. lights out bugle and slept the sleep of the contented.

Shortly before leaving Phet Buri for another compound, I came down with the worst attack of malaria I experienced during our captivity. This illness was so severe that for the first time as a POW I suspected that I might not survive. For seventeen consecutive days, a new malaria siege hit me at mid-morning with heavy, bone-wrenching chills followed by a temperature that reached 107 degrees. The chills that precede the fever of malaria are overwhelming. Cold penetrates every fiber of the body. There is no way to get warm. A victim, having borrowed as many blankets as possible from friends and neighbors, would nonetheless lie for an hour or more huddled beneath this pile, shaking and shivering uncontrollably. When the chill subsided, the heat would come on and soon the victim was feverish.

A week or ten days into this debilitating assault, I began to wonder if it would ever end. As had been the case during most of our incarceration, no medication was available. I became desperate for an end to the siege, and for the first time decided to humble myself and plead for assistance from our captors.

A Japanese guard who worked with me during my carpentry days had been somewhat friendly. I sought him out and asked if he had any quinine, explaining my continued attacks of malaria. He expressed a modest amount of sympathy, but said he had no quinine and couldn't do anything for me. I dejectedly returned to my bunk and literally sweated out the remaining days of my illness. When the attacks let up, I was a weakened wreck and could barely walk. I must have lost fifteen or twenty pounds — and at the time I had precious little to spare.

An attack of malaria normally lasts about three days. After the initial chills pass, the fever lingers for about twenty-four hours, usually breaking on the third day. The victim is left in a weakened state for about a day, then returns to "normal." I do not know how I survived this seventeen-day attack. Its lingering effects dogged me until after our liberation.

The pernicious effects of my malaria eroded the buoyant self-confidence that had helped me ride out my ordeal. Throughout the trials of the past three years I had remained quite optimistic, both about my own ability to survive whatever the Japanese threw at us, and about an early end to the war. My little mental game of envisioning liberation just three short months away had gone on for three long years.

My brush with death at Phet Buri hit me mentally as well as physically. Slowly, pessimism invaded the ramparts of my faith and I began to doubt my ability to survive. The "three months and the war will be over" self-assurances deserted me, and I began wondering if the war would ever end. Were we doomed to forever languish under the Jap's thumb?

Sometime in May 1945, the Japanese again shifted prisoners. I wound up at a camp near Rat Buri, Thailand, which would prove to be my last POW compound. By this time our small American group of prisoners had been split several times, and there must have been less than a hundred of us at Rat Buri. Our officers had been placed in separate camps months before, and every time we were shifted to new camps, some would be left behind, too ill to move. Others were either sent back to the big compound in Singapore, or to Saigon. The Japanese had intended to move most of those on to Japan, but Allied bombers and submarines were now so dominant that nothing could safely move over land or sea.

Shortly after we arrived at Rat Buri, a new group of prisoners were brought in and I was reunited with John Branchflower.

His contingent arrived around noon one day, and I shared my bit of rice with him. He was exhausted from the trip, and ravenously hungry. We were together again until liberation.

The final few weeks of internment began under a cloud of uncertainty. Work parties continued to go out daily, although most of the time I remained in camp, too weak to do much labor. Branchflower and I would pass the time talking or playing cribbage or gin rummy. Somehow, we still had a few sets of playing cards around, although after more than three years of service they were in pitiful shape.

As had been the case during most of our captivity, somewhere in one of the POW compounds, someone had harbored a clandestine radio, and we managed to keep up to date on the progress of the war. We knew by this time, for instance, that the European war had ended and the Japanese were fighting – alone – the final battles of a lost cause.

Our major concern, however, was that the Allies would have to invade and recapture the vast areas of Southeast Asia still occupied by Nippon. Rumors circulated that the Japanese had orders to kill all prisoners should the Allies land invasion forces in the area. After the war, these rumors were confirmed when captured Japanese documents revealed the murder of prisoners to be part of their final strategy.

At Rat Buri, the Japanese permitted us to construct a theater on the parade ground opposite our row of bamboo huts. A few dramas were presented, but our operation never reached the professional level attained at Tamarkan. With the absence of Frank Brydges, none of the scenery came up to the standards established under his hand. Usually I was too weak to do much, although Branchflower resumed his roles in some presentations.

Toward the middle of 1945, the days seemed to drag along. Our guards often appeared quite nervous, and acted as if they wanted as little direct contact with us as necessary to maintain the proper control. Working parties still went out daily, but physical punishment came to a virtual halt. Our captors must have known that the end was near, and they had begun worrying about their own fate.

World War II ended on August 15, 1945, with Japanese acceptance of the unconditional surrender demands made by the Allies. We did not know it at the time, but it was the dropping of atom bombs on Hiroshima and Nagasaki that finally brought the Imperial Japanese forces to their knees. As heinous as nuclear war appears to most of the world today, those two atom bombs saved the lives of untold millions of Japanese soldiers and civilians, as well as Allied troops. They permitted thousands of prisoners held by Nippon to survive. Without them, many of us would have been slaughtered as the Allies fought to liberate occupied territory.

Imprisoned in Japan since late 1942, the Lost Battalion group headed by Captain L. L. Zeigler of Wichita Falls — which included my own section sergeant, Jess Stanbrough — learned of the war's end on the very day of surrender from the same radio that had been carried all the way from Java.

On August 15, 1945, the POWs in Japan were told that the emperor was to make an unprecedented nationwide radio address that day — an astonishing occurrence to the Japanese who looked on their emperor as a god. Japanese guards took Zeigler and his group into nearby tunnels in the belief that it would be a sacrilege for them to even hear Hirohito's voice.

"Prisoners not allowed to hear him talk," a guard named Sancho explained to Stanbrough.

When the surrender was announced, Stanbrough said euphoria overtook the POW compound.

"Even though the civilians were stunned," he said, "they were just about as glad it was over as we were."

Many years later, when Emperor Hirohito made a trip to the United States, he came to the Woods Hole Oceanographic Institute at Woods Hole, Massachusetts, where Stanbrough worked. American authorities would not allow him to be present at any of the functions involving the emperor. "I guess they were afraid I might attack him," Stanbrough said.

In Thailand, work parties went out from our camp as usual on August 15, but returned that afternoon earlier than normal. Rumors flew from barracks to barracks that the war was over, but most of us were simply unable to believe them. The next morning, work parties went out to their regular sites, milling around the trucks and doing nothing for a couple of hours. A Japanese officer drove up in a command car and told the guards to reload the prisoners and return them to camp. Everybody kept saying, "The war is over! The war must be over!" But my pessimism remained intact, and I refused to believe.

All that day, our guards stayed outside the compound, refusing to make contact with us. The air was charged and we huddled about in groups, trying to figure out what was going on.

On the morning of August 17, we received instructions to assemble on the parade ground for an announcement. The ulcer on my right leg had flared up again, and I had trouble walking. Branchflower had helped me make a crude crutch from two pieces of bamboo, and I used the crutch to hobble out to the parade ground with everybody else.

Our Japanese commandant, a lieutenant whose name is lost, slowly walked to the front of the assembly. He stood there for a moment, silently gazing at the ragged formation of British, Australians, Dutch, and Americans who once had been part of a proud military. His audience was a few thousands POWs who were nothing but skin and bone. Most of us ranged in weight from about 80 to 115 pounds. There was nothing to indicate any cultural differences among us. We were all but naked; our captors had never given us any clothing. Many of us stood or leaned on comrades, wearing nothing but g-strings.

The commandant looked down at the ground for a long time, then raised his head, straining to maintain his composure. He spoke in broken English:

> The war is over. The Allies have been victorious. I have been instructed that my soldiers will be responsible for your safekeeping until your own people can repatriate you. Your officers will be reunited with you, and I ask you to cooperate so there will be no additional suffering or bloodshed.

He turned to his right and briskly walked outside the camp to a cluster of small buildings that housed the compound guards.

We stood there as if suspended in infinity. There was not a sound for several minutes. Shock permeated our brains, and slowly we turned to look at one another. Tears began streaming down our cheeks as we realized that the end had come.

We began yelling and jumping up and down. We alternately hugged each other, then stood for a time, speechless. The war was over! We had survived and we would be going home! The impact was almost too much to comprehend. All that suffering — all that dying — all that work and misery were over.

Most of us milled about the parade ground for half an hour or more, then slowly drifted back to our pallets. That afternoon, our officers were reunited with us, and we began roughly reforming into the units that had governed our lives before capture.

The following day, trucks driven by local residents arrived with loads of food and a new issue of clothing. We each got what appeared to be American army-issue trousers, a shirt, underwear, and a pair of boots. They were the most magnificent clothes I had ever seen.

Branchflower and I began talking about what we would do when we returned home. He had been separated from his wife and two daughters for more than four years. I could think of nothing but going back to Wichita Falls, which at the time seemed to be paradise, and of resuming the life of a carefree teenager. But I was no longer a teenager. I was twenty-three years old, having "celebrated" four birthdays in captivity.

Occasionally, my thoughts floated back deep into the Burma jungle to the 80 Kilo hospital camp. I saw the faces of Jimmy Alexander, Frank Faulkner, and Harry Kitchings and I would weep quietly at their loss. I had survived, but they, and tens of thousands of others like them, had not. It did not seem fair. They had given all they had, and theirs had been a short and incomplete life in return. Then, the anticipation of getting out, of surviving the odds and of being able to go free again, would shove grief to the back of my mind. But it always lingered back there. It still does.

"I wonder if my lassies have changed much," Branchflower said one day during our endless discussions about going home. "Pauline was only a wee bonny the last time I saw her. And I still haven't set eyes on the baby. They won't even know who I am. Maybe they will be too frightened to have anything to do with me."

"Well, maybe they will at first, but I bet it won't take you too

long to smother them with hugs and kisses and they'll finally
know their daddy has come home," I replied.

During these last weeks, the Japanese had requested that we
remain inside our compound. We were glad to oblige, wishing to
do nothing that might bring on an incident before our own
forces could come to Thailand to reclaim us. A couple of Americans in the camp came up with enough red, white, and blue material to stitch together an American flag about two feet wide and
four feet long. We confiscated a flagpole inside the camp that
had been used to fly the Rising Sun, and ran the wonderful red,
white, and blue to the top. We cheered and cheered, until our
voices were hoarse.

The noise attracted the attention of our Japanese commandant; he later asked us to take the flag down since there still were
hordes of armed Japanese soldiers stationed in the area.

"Japanese soldiers see American flag and maybe get upset
and fire rifle," he said. "If you please, take it down so no trouble
comes."

We complied. We routinely saw hundreds of armed Japanese soldiers marching past our camp, and the risk, we concluded, was too great; nothing should be placed ahead of our
safely returning home. There was, however, no more flying of the
Japanese flag in our compound either. We were delighted to see
the hated symbol we called the "flaming ass-hole" disappear.

A few days before our small contingent of American POWs
left our final prison camp, we heard from a nearby compound a
chilling story. Three British prisoners there, to celebrate the end
of their captivity, bartered with a Thai family at a neighboring village for two liters of homemade rice whiskey — "white lightning."

That evening, the three got roaring drunk and had to be carried to their bunks. The next morning all three were dead. They
had survived forty-two months of hell only to die by their own
hand on the eve of freedom.

August 31, 1945, proved to be our last night in a Japanese
POW camp. While we had essentially been under the command of
our own officers for the two weeks since the war's end, Japanese
guards had remained outside the compound, keeping a wary eye
on us, whom they still considered their charges.

That evening we prepared our final prison camp meal. Our rations had greatly improved in the days since hostilities ceased, but we still relied on rice as the basic ingredient of our meals. I took my mess kit, loaded with rice and a stew that contained real meat, and made my way to the next hut, where Branchflower and his fellow British soldiers were quartered.

We ate in silence for a time. Then John said, "Well, I'm ready for this thing to end. When do you think we should be going home?"

"I don't really know," I replied. "But I'm ready for some good old American food. I think I've had enough rice to last me the rest of my life!"

"You think you will ever eat any rice when you get home?" he asked.

"I'm not sure I'll ever want to, although it tastes pretty good when you don't have anything else," I replied. There was a pause as we sat in thought on the edge of the bamboo platform where Branchflower slept.

"I sure can remember, though, back in the jungles when I wanted a lot more rice than was available," John said quietly. Our minds wandered back to the Burma jungles — the horrors we had known there. "Maybe I'll have some rice back home just to remember how it was."

"Maybe I will too."

Back in Bicycle Camp, Noel Mason had said, "You and I are going to have to eat a thousand cups of rice before we get home. Maybe even more." Sitting there on John Branchflower's tattered bunk, I finished my thousandth cup of rice.

Orders came on September 1, 1945, for all Americans in the camp to assemble near the front gate. Trucks were waiting to take us on the first leg to freedom!

Branchflower and I held a hurried conference, which turned out to be our last time together. We again exchanged addresses (his was 49 Lincoln Street, Patricroft, Winton, Manchester, England) and vowed to keep in touch. Just before we loaded in the trucks, John handed me the picture of him, his wife, and eldest daughter, and said, "Don't forget us."

"We have a friendship I don't want to end here," I told him. "Let's really keep in touch. I want to meet your family someday. I really want to see you again." Tears filled my eyes as we shook hands, and I joined our group at the gate. We loaded into the trucks, and began the three-hour drive to Bangkok.

That was the last contact I had with John Branchflower. I began writing him shortly after returning to the States, but never heard from him again. Years later, when my wife and I went to London on vacation, I tried every avenue I could think of in an effort to run him down, but never found a trace of him. I also wrote several letters to Frank Brydges, in care of the Sydney *Daily Herald,* but this, too, proved futile. It would be thirty-six years after the war that I would be reunited with Frank at his home in Sydney. It was a glorious reunion. My wife and I took the train in downtown Sydney out to the suburbs where Frank lived, and he met us at the station. We drove to his house and had dinner with Frank and his wife, and spent several hours reliving the good old days at Tamarkan. Frank died about three years after our reunion of complications from heart disease.

After more than three years of captivity, the staggering fact that we actually were free had a profound effect on me. I recall the major events of those days, but the details are caught up in a hazy swirl of confusion. I must have suffered from a moderate amount of psychological shock, and found it hard to adjust to what was going on. Weeks later, in Washington state, I would be riding a bus, or eating at a restaurant, and feel as if I were an alien, a being from another planet. I just couldn't adjust to being a normal human again for some time.

Having left our last POW camp in Thailand, we arrived in Bangkok and spent the night on cots in a warehouse. The next day, September 2, we boarded trucks for a ride to the main city airport where American C-47s were waiting to fly us out. I remember boarding for my very first airplane ride. I also recall meeting a woman who must have been some type of stewardess, but I was unable to carry on a conversation — she was the first woman any of us had been around in nearly four years.

The pilot turned out to be a twenty-three-year-old who had received his pilot training at Sheppard Air Force Base, Wichita

Falls — my hometown. The entire air force crew on the plane that took us to freedom did everything possible to make our flight pleasant. The pilot invited us one at a time up front to the co-pilot's seat. We must have been flying at no more than two thousand feet, and while I was sitting beside the pilot, he spotted a Thai farmer below us plowing his rice paddy with a team of oxen.

"Let's have a little fun," the pilot said to me.

He pushed the stick forward, and we began a slow dive toward the rice farmer. As we swooped only a few hundred feet above the hapless fellow, he dived into the mud as his oxen team bolted across the paddy, with the plow churning up the mud behind. We laughed and laughed, but later I often thought of the trouble this poor farmer must have had reclaiming his team and resuming his cultivation.

We stopped briefly at an air base near Rangoon, Burma, then resumed our flight to Dum Dum, a huge Allied air base at Calcutta, India, where there was a large U.S. Army general hospital.

It was so hard to fully accept the fact that we were free — that we were actually alive and back with our own people. At the Calcutta hospital, our clothing was taken away and burned. We were deloused, washed, and scrubbed, and checked into a hospital bed. It was most difficult to learn to eat real food again. So many things brought on nausea. I was unable to eat anything with salt — we had been on a salt-free diet for forty-two months. Anything with chocolate made me ill.

My recollection of events over the next few weeks is somewhat unclear. Our medical people did everything possible to make our recovery pleasant. We went through numerous interviews designed to integrate us back into our own armed forces. I must have spent a week to ten days in Calcutta before doctors decided I was fit to travel back to the States. In the meantime, I received a telegram from my father, who had moved from Texas to Seattle, Washington, early in the war. After learning my family now lived in Washington, I decided to return there. Madigan General Hospital, at Fort Lewis, Washington, near the city of Tacoma, was the nearest medical facility, so I chose it as my destination.

The army began processing repatriated POWs on an individual basis. When I was released to travel, I was issued orders that allowed me to take any form of transportation available to Fort Lewis. POWs were given a "Project J" designation that placed us on a very high priority for travel. The United States had twelve million men in uniform during the Second World War, and most of them were overseas when it ended. It became a massive job just to get all of them back. It was difficult for everybody, except those of us on the Project J list, to get a seat on a plane or a berth on a ship going home. My priority served me well. On the way home, at Cairo, Egypt, I was walking up the steps to enter a transport plane and met a general coming down the steps. When I took my seat, a passenger next to me said, "I guess you know you just bumped a general to get that seat." I just grinned and kept silent. I was so anxious to get back I didn't care who got bumped.

I departed Dum Dum air base on September 12 at 1:18 P.M. Our flight home took us through Agra, another base in India, then to Karachi, Baghdad, Cairo, Tripoli, Casablanca, the Azores, Newfoundland, and then America, arriving in New York City at 6:05 A.M. the next day.

I stopped over a couple of days in an army hospital in the New York area, and was surprised to find German POWs serving as orderlies there. Their health surpassed mine at least a hundred fold, but somehow it pleased me to see them doing so well.

My last leg home took me by train across the northern tier of states from New York to Seattle. The only space available was in a coach, and I sat or slept leaning against a window for the four-day trip. I took a taxi from the station to my parents' home in the Seattle suburbs, arriving unannounced. They knew I was on my way home, but did not know when I would arrive.

It was a very emotional reunion. My youngest brother and sister were still at home, and they clung to me like magnets. Within hours my mother was complaining of the shortages they had suffered during the war. For some reason this seemed to have a mollifying effect on me and finally I realized that I really was home. It was over! And I had survived, beaten war and pestilence and a hated enemy who had done his best to kill me.

I entered the Southeast Asian war an immature nineteen-year-old who had sought his first experience with the military for the few dollars in pay given National Guardsmen in the late 1930s — a hedge against the poverty of the Great Depression. Along with the money came experiences and friendships that deepened as we trained and fought as a unit, and persevered as prisoners of war. Our little group of Texans emerged much wiser from our experiences, eager to return to the civilized world that we had left so long in the past.

The years of captivity were costly. We left so many of our friends in shallow graves in the jungles. We who survived can never fully recover. The scars — on body and mind — are lasting.

Epilogue

WHEN THE MEN of the 2d Battalion, 131st Field Artillery, became prisoners of war, they could not know the immensity of the oncoming clash of two fundamentally diverse cultures. On one hand were not quite a thousand Americans — mostly Texans from rural or small-town communities, many still of high school age — who had joined the National Guard to help get them through the Depression. They were led by officers who were not professional soldiers and had between them little or no leadership training. No one had expected to go to war.

On the other hand were their Asian captors, whose culture had taught them that the ends justified the means, that the individual was nothing, that he had no rights other than those promoting the nation's goals and Hideki Tojo's designs. It was acceptable to lie, cheat, or degrade fellow humans if that furthered the "cause." These traits would reappear in the decades following the war as the Japanese set out to dominate world markets.

The postwar period found the United States the only country with its economy, populace, and infrastructure healthy enough to sponsor worldwide recovery. Europe was battered by nearly six years of war. The major cities of the Nazi empire were bombed to rubble. There was no government in Europe capable of ruling.

The Japanese island empire was in virtually the same state. The Old World lay prostrate.

Instead of punishing old enemies who had tried to destroy them, Americans opened their hearts and pocketbooks, pouring money, materials, and even manpower into a massive reconstruction. We were immensely successful. Within a decade, both the German and the Japanese people were back on their feet — and their economies followed.

Japanese economic warlords took advantage of the free-trade policy practices of the United States to introduce their products, often at prices below costs — a strategy designed to eliminate competition. Our government simply did not know how to deal with the Asian philosophy of business, and we practically rolled over and played dead while the Japanese trade cartels, backed solidly by their government, moved in and killed off millions of American jobs by undercutting and underselling U.S. manufacturers. At the same time, the Japanese closed their markets to U.S. products, refusing to let us do business there. Our government spent decades in useless trade negotiations — often seeming to have reached an agreement with our competitors, only to see the Japanese renege on their "word."

Japanese negotiators smiled broadly, bowed profusely and agreed to anything, only to return home to resume their one-way business practices. The Japanese understood competition well. Frequently they played the game alone, American and European markets choosing not to compete — out of faith in the old ways, or simple complacency.

The prewar Japanese military code was something right out of the Middle Ages. The officer corps was well-trained. They worshiped the Emperor as their god and literally had the power of life or death over the soldiers under their command. Their code was uncompromising, and they were required to commit suicide rather than surrender. It was by this code that Allied prisoners of war were perceived as contemptable, undeserving of dignified — or even humane — treatment. The Japanese never understood mass surrenders, such as those conducted by the Dutch government in Java, or the British at Singapore.

When the war ended, 166 members of the 2d Battalion and

the USS *Houston* had died in prison camps. Of this number, ninety-nine died at 80 Kilo and 100 Kilo camps. Virtually all of these deaths came in 1943 during the worst of the heavy labor on the Death Railway in Burma.

On Christmas Day, 1978, Doctor Henri Hekking instituted an affidavit, signed in The Hague, Netherlands, supporting survivors of the 2d Battalion and the *Houston* who were having trouble convincing the U.S. Veterans Administration that they were suffering from complex service-connected illnesses:

Let me start with a description of the general camp conditions and the treatment of the POW along the different camps in Burma. Most camps consisted of miserable huts, built by the POW from bamboo, dry twigs and leaves and hardly giving protection against the tough climate conditions. The dry season was dry indeed, with just enough water for cooking and seldom for body cleaning. I remember quite well that on many places the dust was 20 to 30 centimeters thick. The wet season was damp and cold and really wet. The dust changed into a sticky mud, that made walking and working extremely hard and tiring, and I have seen many chronic[ally] sick men, forced to join the daily labor parties, completely exhausted after the relative short walk from the camp to the working area.

The tropical rain showers were a great nuisance because the roofs of the huts were leaking like a basket. The latrines were long, open ditches teeming with grub[s] and millions of hatching "blue bottles"; the flies looking after the spread of the germs!

The treatment of the POW by the Japanese and Korean guards was a mere shame.

Although three-quarters of the camp population was permanently ill, the guards would allow only 15 per cent no-duty on account of disease. If you had only a little more missing on the morning parade, a beating for the missing patients and for the doctor ensued.

"No work, no food," said the guard; so there were no rations for no-duty people.

The food: The supply from the hinterland before the railway was finished was entirely insufficient.

Our daily food consisted of old, musty, by bugs completely decorticated rice and a little salt. Sometimes, but so seldom that it was negligible, there was a little meat unfit for consumption by the Japanese soldiers, and a bit of pumpkin, just enough to divide among some very emaciated patients.

As already mentioned there was an abundance of flies in the camps and it was difficult to eat your rice without swallowing some living flies at the same time.

From the medical viewpoint, there are some crucial camp conditions to be mentioned, especially from the Burma period, lasting for more than a year:

1. The heavy labor under exceptional climatological influences, ranging from unbearable heat to periods of cold, tropical rains; the constant emotional stress and the fear for unexpected punishment by the guards. The living in [un]sanitary, overcrowded huts (60 centimeters per man) ideal for the promotion of tuberculosis and other pulmonary infections. In many camps normal sleep was impossible by [because of] the armies of body lice and bedbugs that fed upon the emaciated bodies.

2. The food consisted of mere carbohydrates with no vitamins and no fat, and only small traces of unfit (not derived from animal food) proteins. The dubious value of even this entirely deficient diet was still more diminished by the diarrhoea [that caused] rapid bowel movement.

3. The whole range of infectious and deficiency diseases, especially the enteric conditions with profuse diarrhoea, from which practically everybody suffered [sic]. The absence of mosquito nets and quinine caused real epidemics of malaria. Although in the beginning – in spite of [the] lack of indispensable nutrients – the body's reserves and regulatory systems could maintain homeostasis for some time; finally they broke down by inanition and the body started to consume its own cells and tissues, with consequently much irreparable damage. What damage has been done to the intricate system of the many enzymes, necessary to maintain life,

one can only guess. There probably won't be a single tissue or vital organ not badly affected for life by all the influences mentioned above.

At a rough estimate, I have the firm conviction that the mortality by all different causes, in the Burma group, is markedly greater than the national average; the same applies to diseases and medical disabilities as well.

Even if a direct link between incidents during POW time and the present ailments is not clearly detectable, the possibility never can be denied that this ailment only could find expression in a body weakened by the tremendous impact of the POW time, and this also means war connected.

[Author's note] The above-mentioned statements are confirmed by countless articles in the international medical press and in the great textbooks of medicine.

For October 23, 1945, some of the families of 2d Battalion soldiers organized a gigantic welcome home celebration at Wichita Falls, Texas. Virtually every survivor able to walk gathered for that gala, and the battalion formed by units marched down Scott Street in the heart of Wichita Falls.

Tens of thousands of family members and friends lined Scott Street. For the men of the Lost Battalion, it was the culmination of their dreams of returning home. This first reunion was dedicated to the 2d Battalion, 131st Field Artillery — the "Texas Lost Battalion" as the media had dubbed it when it disappeared.

Since family members back home had not been aware of the existence of the 369 USS *Houston* survivors who had joined the 2d Battalion in POW camps, those survivors had not been invited to the initial reunion in 1945. The Lost Battalion decided to make the reunions permanent, meeting each year on a weekend nearest August 15, the date of the Japanese surrender. For the 1946 reunion, a large number of navy and Marine survivors of the *Houston* were invited, and that group decided to become permanent members of the Lost Battalion Association.

A large number of the returning Lost Battalion survivors had entered the military in 1940, either just out of high school or even before graduating, and few had the training to return to civilian life and make a living. What they found, though, was the greatest gift possible for their future — the GI Bill, offering them money for a wide range of education, including the pursuit of college degrees.

While some members chose to remain in the military as a career, hundreds of others took advantage of the GI Bill and enrolled in college. They successfully pursued careers in law, engineering, teaching, business, government, and journalism.

The few who had been married before departing for war returned to resume their interrupted lives. Some, however, found that their wives had deserted them and remarried. Most of us who had been teenagers when we left were fortunate enough to find lifelong mates and were married within a year of returning.

In my own case, I remained in the army until July 28, 1946, when I was declared physically well enough to leave the service. During the October 1945 reunion in Wichita Falls, I began dating Vivian Marie Carter, whose family and mine had attended the same Baptist church when we were younger. We were married on May 19, 1946, in Wichita Falls.

Upon being discharged at Fort Lewis, Washington, I returned to Wichita Falls and enrolled in Midwestern State University (then known as Hardin College) in the fall. Aptitude tests administered by the army indicated that I was best suited for a writing career, so my studies turned toward journalism. I was also guided into this field by a marvelous teacher at Hardin College, Dr. Madge Davis, who headed the Department of English and Journalism. The college did not offer a degree in journalism, so I chose history as my major, with minors in English and journalism.

The late Curtis Cook, who was managing editor of the morning newspaper in Wichita Falls, the *Record-News,* also was a journalism teacher at Hardin College, and we hit it off from the start. I did well in his classes, and went to work for the *Record-News* as a cub reporter in April 1949 — four months before receiving my bachelor of arts degree in August. During my three years in college, the first two of our three daughters were born — Linda on February 27, 1947, and Kay on April 19, 1949. Our third daughter, Janis Kyle, was born February 26, 1957, at Baylor Medical Center in Dallas.

After nearly three years at my hometown newspaper, I was offered a job in Dallas with the United Press (now United Press

International). I worked at the Dallas UP office until the summer of 1958, when I was transferred to Houston to operate the one-person office there for four years.

The decades of the fifties and sixties were booming days in America. The influx of twelve million military personnel back into the economy was successfully completed, and it was this generation that helped usher in the greatest standard of living the world had ever seen.

During my stint with UP in Houston, that area grew at a staggering rate. The region contained more than 40 percent of the world's petrochemical industry. Houston got the Manned Spacecraft Center — the nation's space headquarters — and saw the introduction of major league baseball and football, as well as the world's first indoor major sports center — the Astrodome. My one-man office grew to three writers and a full-time photographer to handle all the news Houston produced.

My Houston assignment with UP saw my horizons expand dramatically. During my four years there, I coordinated the coverage of two major hurricanes; became a member of the Baseball Writers of America, and reported on major sports events: the Houston Open Golf tournament, the Houston Oilers' performance in the American Football League, and the annual Southwest Conference basketball tournament then staged in Houston in late December.

In May 1962, United Press moved me to Austin as the bureau chief of the wire service's Capitol Bureau. The press room at that time was on the second floor of the State Capitol, located between the governor's office and the House of Representatives chamber. It was about the size of the living room in a large home. The entire press corps consisted of only about two dozen reporters and photographers representing the two major wire services and the large Texas newspapers from Dallas, Fort Worth, San Antonio, Austin, and Houston.

Just after taking up my duties in Austin, United Press and the International News Service merged, becoming United Press International (UPI). The merger had little impact on us other than adding a few small daily newspapers to our client list. The end result was the abolition of INS, leaving America with two major news wire services — Associated Press (AP) and UPI.

John Connally had just been elected governor of Texas when I arrived in Austin. He assumed the office in January 1963, and was reelected twice, serving as chief executive for six years. More than a decade later, Texans would change their Constitution to allow four-year terms for the governor and other statewide officials, instead of these two-year stints.

Becoming chief of UPI's Austin office made me the wire service's chief government and political writer. I took naturally to the duties, and government and politics soon became the motivating forces dominating my career.

Connally was a fascinating politician to be around. He was a dynamic governor, and being more or less a political protege of Lyndon Baines Johnson, Connally's influence was not limited to the borders of Texas.

The biggest news story of my career was the assassination of President John F. Kennedy in Dallas on November 22, 1963. My initiation into national politics as a professional writer actually began during the 1960 presidential election.

While UPI had regular personnel who traveled with national political figures, local staffers become involved when these officials come to their home territories. I was initially exposed to Kennedy when he came to Houston to tackle head-on the touchy and crucial issue of the separation of church and state. Kennedy was a member of the Catholic Church, and a Catholic had never before been elected president of the United States.

Many Protestants, especially Baptists, were suspicious that a Catholic president would allow the Pope to unduly influence the decision-making process in Washington. To put the issue to rest, Kennedy agreed to hold a meeting in Houston with a group that became known in the national media as "the Baptist preachers."

United Press felt the issue was so crucial that I was instructed to hire a court reporter to record the entire proceedings. We did, and I spent most of the night after the meeting running the transcript on one of our national teletype wires.

That year I also covered a major appearance in Houston by Richard M. Nixon, the Republican presidential nominee. The Kennedy-Johnson ticket prevailed in the November election, and three years later, Dallas, Texas, took its tragic place in U.S. history.

A growing number of Texans were becoming dissatisfied

with Lyndon Johnson. They became embittered when he caved in and accepted the vice presidential nomination offered, without a lot of enthusiasm, by the Kennedys that year.

The growing political fervor became ingrained in my professional life in the early 1960s. The political bug had bitten me and had become the motivating force driving my career.

Growing discontent with the new Kennedy administration became a major political strain after John Goodwin Tower, a Republican and an unknown assistant professor at Midwestern University in Wichita Falls, won the special election in 1961 to succeed Lyndon Johnson, who had become vice president in January. By 1963, Texas Democrats were torn asunder by the growing number of conservatives deserting their party, especially in national elections. Johnson began to fear that his own political machine could not hold together to deliver the state again in the 1964 presidential race, so Kennedy agreed to come to Texas in November 1963 to mend the widening rift.

The presidential caravan was winding its way through downtown Dallas, headed for the Trade Mart for a final rally there before moving on to Austin, when the bullets from Lee Harvey Oswald's high-powered rifle shattered Kennedy's brain and wounded Connally. The presidential limousine fled, carrying them to Parkland Hospital, about a mile away.

I was standing in the UPI Capitol office watching our "A" national news wire when the Dallas UPI office broke in on a story out of Minneapolis being filed by the UPI Chicago office at 12:34 P.M. CST. The Dallas story went like this:

UPI A7N DA
PRECEDE KENNEDY
DALLAS, NOV. 22 (UPI) — THREE SHOTS WERE FIRED AT PRESIDENT KENNEDY'S MOTORCADE TODAY IN DOWNTOWN DALLAS.
JT1234PCS..

The Chicago UPI office tried to resume its Minneapolis story but the New York controlling office came on the wire and told everyone to hold up, commanding "Dallas it is yours."

Atlanta then tried to break in, but New York again told everybody to stay off the wire, turning it again over to Dallas, which filed the next news of the shooting:

UPI A8N DA
URGENT
1ST ADD SHOTS, DALLAS (A7N) XXX DOWNTOWN DALLAS.
NO CASUALTIES WERE REPORTED.
THE INCIDENT OCCURRED NEAR THE COUNTY SHERIFF'S OFFICE ON MAIN STREET, JUST EAST OF AN UNDERPASS LEADING TOWARD THE TRADE MART WHERE THE PRESIDENT WAS TO MA
FLASH
FLASH
KENNEDY SERIOUSLY WOUNDED
PERHAPS SERIOUSLY
PERHAPS FATALLY BY ASSASSINS BULLET
JT1239PCS..

That was how the first word of the Kennedy assassination made it out to the public. I instinctively knew that I had to get to Dallas. I knew that they would need all the help they could get up there. The Dallas shootings obviously eliminated the big Austin finale that had been planned for the presidential visit.

I telephoned my wife. Both of us were in tears as we consoled each other in the face of the unbelievable. I told her I was headed for Dallas, and drove directly to the Austin airport where I got the last seat available on the next Braniff flight to Love Field in Dallas. Our plane was the first to land there after *Air Force One* had departed for Washington, carrying the new president, Lyndon B. Johnson, along with the body of his slain predecessor.

I spent most of the next four days at Parkland Hospital where I was assigned to keep watch on the gravely wounded Connally. I was there when the Dallas office informed me that Oswald had been shot and was en route to Parkland. I stood in the corridor at the emergency entrance as they wheeled his still, pale body to the trauma center. It was obvious that Oswald had been fatally wounded – he appeared to be dead when they rushed past where I was standing.

Connally recovered from his wounds and I resumed my duties in Austin. Later, I would serve as his press secretary the last year he was in office. I returned to UPI shortly after Connally left office, but was back at my old job only a couple of years when Senator Tower, who was up for reelection in 1972, lured me again into the political world. I quit UPI for the last time January 1, 1972, and took on the job of press secretary to the Tower reelection staff. We won over Democrat Barefoot Sanders that fall, and I moved to Washington as the senator's press secretary.

A little "two bit" burglary that became known as Watergate had just been revealed as Tower took the oath of office for his third term in the United States Senate. We settled into our crowded space in 142 Old Senate Office Building and operated routinely for a few months while Watergate festered into a full-blown political hurricane. Soon it dominated every facet of government in the nation's capital. The entire governmental apparatus came to a halt while the Nixon administration broadened its efforts to cover up. The efforts failed and Nixon resigned just before impeachment overcame him. Gerald Ford became president.

The whole Watergate mess thoroughly disgusted me with the Washington scene, and my family and I became restless to return to Texas. I was offered a political appointment as regional director of a small agency then a part of the Department of Defense. It was known as the Defense Civil Preparedness Agency, with its headquarters in an underground federal center at Denton, thirty-five miles north of Dallas and Fort Worth. I served in that position for five years, until a reorganization changed it to the Federal Emergency Management Agency (FEMA).

After two years working for a friend in Dallas, I accepted an offer as editorial page editor of the *Fort Worth Star-Telegram*, serving in that capacity until retiring on August 1, 1987.

My wife and I moved back to Austin as our retirement residence as I felt I could remain somewhat active in politics there. Since retiring, I have been involved in two campaigns with Kent Hance for the Texas Railroad Commission, one for him when he ran for governor, and one race with Rick Perry for state agriculture commissioner, where we successfully ousted that controversial populist, Jack Hightower.

During the early years of the 1990s, I became a volunteer teacher of journalism for junior high school students at Hyde Park Baptist High School. I look on this as a challenge to try to encourage young people to become interested in what is going on around the world, and to especially take an interest in government and politics. It is a most fascinating subject which, sadly, is virtually ignored by a large segment of the American public. Too bad for them. Too bad for us.

At the Lost Battalion convention in San Antonio in August 1993, my comrades elected me as the executive secretary — there was no one else on the scene willing to accept the position. The executive secretary is responsible for publishing and mailing four or five newsletters annually to our list containing about 530 names. It also entails keeping the Lost Battalion roster current, and trying to keep up with what our group, which is scattered across the nation, is doing.

It is not an unpleasant task for, to paraphrase Winston Churchill in one of his famous World War II talks, it permits me to give back to my comrades, who have devoted a lot of blood, sweat, and tears to their association. I was reminded of how it is the good things that really sustain us while preparing the April 1994 Lost Battalion Newsletter, which we dedicated to our late and deeply missed friend, Dr. Henri H. Hekking, who died just short of his ninety-first birthday on January 29, 1994. On his very first visit with our group at its 1976 reunion in Lubbock, Dr. Hekking told us:

> Let us try not to be too bitter about all the hardships of war days of long ago, and let us try to remember only the good things. And among those good things, the very best is that thanks to the prisoner times, we got a foundation of this Lost Battalion Association, one of the most beautiful and best organizations of ex-POWs in the United States, I know that for sure. I got this from different people. Try to keep your Lost Battalion Association healthy, young, and strong. And may God bless you all, my friends.

IMPERIAL JAPANESE ARMY

Date Oct May 1944

Your ~~mail (and~~) ~~are received with thanks.~~

My health is (good, ~~usual~~, ~~poor~~).

~~I am ill in hospital.~~

~~I am working for pay (I am paid monthly salary).~~

I am not working.

My best regards to FAMILY AND FRIENDS

Yours ever,

F.O. Thompson

The postcard completed by Thompson in Java, in October 1942, and finally delivered by an excited postman on Christmas Eve, 1943. Recognizing that the incorrect date was written in a hand other than her sons, Thompson's mother wrote atop the card, "Notice this date on this one he didn't write that."

Kyle Thompson at age seventeen, shortly after he enlisted in the Texas National Guard, 36th Division, at Wichita Falls, Texas, in 1939.

Twelve-foot by twelve-foot tents which housed soldiers of the 36th Division at Camp Bowie, Brownwood, Texas, after mobilization in November 1940.

Command car which carried radio equipment during the year of training at Camp Bowie and later during combat against overwhelming
Japanese forces in Java.

Left to right, Wilson G. "Dub" Reed and Wilbur Rockett, members of the Regimental Head-quarters Battery radio crew, on the back of an army truck being transported to new field positions during maneuvers in Texas in 1941.

Technical Sergeant Jess H. Stanbrough outside a troop train on November 11, 1941, leaving Camp Bowie for unknown destination "Plum." While Plum turned out to be the Philippines, the group never arrived there as their troop ship was midway across the Pacific Ocean when the Japanese bombed Pearl Harbor on December 7, 1941, forcing a diversion to Australia.

The USS *Republic*, a World War I–era troop transport, which carried members of the 2d Battalion, 131st Field Artillery, and other troops across the Pacific and ultimately to Brisbane, Australia, arriving there just before Christmas 1941.

The SS *Bloemfontein*, on which the 131st FA shipped from Brisbane to Surabaya, Java's main port. During the tense passage, the Dutch captain played Viennese waltzes and Gershwin's "Rhapsody in Blue" on the ship's public address system.

One of the 75mm guns of E Battery, apparently stored in Surabaya by the Japanese and found after the war by the returning Netherlands Marines, who used it to mark the entrance of their barracks on Java.

Major bridge being constructed in early 1943 across Kwae Noi River, also known as the River Kwai.

Major cuts through rocky hills and mountains.

Various scenes showing cuts, bridges, and passes through rugged jungle country.

Various scenes showing cuts, bridges, and passes through rugged jungle country.

Various scenes showing cuts, bridges, and passes through rugged jungle country.

Various scenes showing cuts, bridges, and passes through rugged jungle country.

Allied bombers drop explosives on the steel railway bridge spanning the Kwae Noi River, also known as the River Kwai, in 1944. The bridge was built with Allied prisoner of war labor. The POW compound, *left*, is Tamarkan, where thousands of prisoners were housed after completion of the infamous Death Railway in Burma and Thailand. — AWM negative #118877.

The theater on the middle parade grounds in the Allied POW camp at Tamarkan, which was near the north bank of the Kwae Noi River. Note the prisoner on stage dressed only in a g-string cloth, common apparel after nearly three years as prisoners of the Japanese army. — AWM negative #157871

A typical prisoner of war camp in Burma and Thailand on the Death Railway. This picture is of a camp in the Burma jungles and shows Allied POWs in various states of "jungle dress" outside their bamboo and grass barracks. — AWM negative #157870

Lance Corporal John Branchflower, of the British Army, his wife, Leah, and their eldest daughter, Pauline, just before he shipped out for North Africa, and later for Singapore, where he was captured with his unit by the Japanese in early 1942. Branchflower and the author became good friends in the Tamarkan POW compound in 1944.

Kyle Thompson, *right*, at the section of a wall in Jakarta (Batavia), Indonesia, housing the main entrance of the first prisoner of war camp for the 131st Field Artillery and survivors of the USS *Houston* after their capture by the Japanese in March 1942. With him are two fellow army radio crew members, Wilson G. "Dub" Reed, *left*, and Jess H. Stanbrough. The trip was with a group of former POWs who made a tour in 1981 of countries where they had been held in prison camps.

Entry to the Kanchanaburi, Thailand, War Cemetery, the final resting place of hundreds of British, Australian, and Dutch prisoners who died building the infamous Death Railway during World War II. *Left*, Otto Schwarz, of Union, NJ, a survivor of the USS *Houston* sunk off the Java coast in 1942; *right* is a Buddhist monk who befriended the group during their 1981 visit.

Philip Gans, of South Plains, NJ, *left*, a survivor of the USS *Houston*, and Mark Summers of Fort Worth, Texas, lay a wreath during the 1981 visit in memory of Allied troops who died while working on the Death Railway in Burma and Thailand.

INSTRUMENT OF SURRENDER

We, acting by command of and in behalf of the Emperor of Japan, the Japanese Government and the Japanese Imperial General Headquarters, hereby accept the provisions set forth in the declaration issued by the heads of the Governments of the United States, China and Great Britain on 26 July 1945, at Potsdam, and subsequently adhered to by the Union of Soviet Socialist Republics, which four powers are hereafter referred to as the Allied Powers.

We hereby proclaim the unconditional surrender to the Allied Powers of the Japanese Imperial General Headquarters and of all Japanese armed forces and all armed forces under Japanese control wherever situated.

We hereby command all Japanese forces wherever situated and the Japanese people to cease hostilities forthwith, to preserve and save from damage all ships, aircraft, and military and civil property and to comply with all requirements which may be imposed by the Supreme Commander for the Allied Powers or by agencies of the Japanese Government at his direction.

We hereby command the Japanese Imperial General Headquarters to issue at once orders to the Commanders of all Japanese forces and all forces under Japanese control wherever situated to surrender unconditionally themselves and all forces under their control.

We hereby command all civil, military and naval officials to obey and enforce all proclamations, orders and directives deemed by the Supreme Commander for the Allied Powers to be proper to effectuate this surrender and issued by him or under his authority and we direct all such officials to remain at their posts and to continue to perform their non-combatant duties unless specifically relieved by him or under his authority.

We hereby undertake for the Emperor, the Japanese Government and their successors to carry out the provisions of the Potsdam Declaration in good faith, and to issue whatever orders and take whatever action may be required by the Supreme Commander for the Allied Powers or by any other designated representative of the Allied Powers for the purpose of giving effect to that Declaration.

We hereby command the Japanese Imperial Government and the Japanese Imperial General Headquarters at once to liberate all allied prisoners of war and civilian internees now under Japanese control and to provide for their protection, care, maintenance and immediate transportation to places as directed.

The authority of the Emperor and the Japanese Government to rule the state shall be subject to the Supreme Commander for the Allied Powers who will take such steps as he deems proper to effectuate these terms of surrender.

APAN at _____
day of _____ SEPTEMBER _____ , 1945.

nd in behalf of the Emperor of Japan
se Government

nd in behalf of the Japanese
l Headquarters.

APAN at __0908__
day of _____ SEPTEMBER _____ , 1945,
China, United Kingdom and the
and in the interests of the other

ander for the Allied Powers.

Union of Soviet Socialist Republics
Representative

Commonwealth of Australia Representative

Dominion of Canada Representative

Provisional Government of the French
Republic Representative

Kingdom of the Netherlands Representative

Dominion of New Zealand Representative

Copy of the Instrument of Surrender ending World War II. It was signed by Allied leaders, including Gen. Douglas MacArthur, and Japanese officials, aboard the USS *Missouri* in Tokyo Bay, Japan, at 9:08 A.M. on September 2, 1945.

At the End of the Day

Composer Unknown

The song, "At the End of the Day," written by an unknown author in
Tamarkan prisoner of war compound in 1944. The song was used in
performances put on by Allied POWs in 1944 and '45, at a bamboo and
banana leaf stage built in the middle parade ground.

Appendix A

It is a great pleasure to me to see you at this place as I am appointed Chief of the war prisoners camp obedient to the Imperial Command issued by His Majesty the Emperor. The great East Asiatic war has broken out due to the rising of the East Asiatic Nations whose hearts were burnt with the desire to live and preserve their nations on account of the intrusion of the British and Americans for the past many years.

There is, therefore, no other reason for Japan to drive out the Anti-Asiatic powers of the arrogant and insolent British and Americans from East Asia in co-operation with our neighbors of China and other East Asiatic Nations and establish the Great East Asia Co-Prosperity Sphere for the benefit of all human beings and establish lasting great peace in the world. During the past few centuries, Nippon has made great sacrifices and extreme endeavors to become the leader of the East Asiatic Nations, who were mercilessly and pitifully treated by the outside forces of the British and Americans, and the Nippon Army, without disgracing anybody, has been doing her best until now for fostering Nippon's real power.

You are only a few remaining skeletons after the invasion of East Asia for the past few centuries, and are pitiful victims. It is

169

not your fault, but until your governments do not *[sic]* wake up
from their dreams and discontinue their resistance, all of you will
not be released. However, I shall not treat you badly for the sake
of humanity as you have no fighting power left at all.

His Majesty the Emperor has been deeply anxious about all
prisoners of war, and has ordered us to enable the operating of
War Prisoner camps at almost all the places in the SW [south-
west] countries.

The Imperial Thoughts are unestimable and the Imperial
Favors are infinite and, as such, you should weep with gratitude
at the greatness of them. I shall correct or mend the misleading
and improper Anti-Japanese ideas. I shall meet with you hereafter and at the beginning I shall require of you the four following
points:

(1)   I heard that you complain about the insufficiency of various items. Although there may be lack of materials it is difficult to meet your requirements. Just turn your eyes to the
present conditions of the world. It is entirely different from
the pre-war times. In all lands and countries materials are
considerably short and it is not easy to obtain even a small
piece of cigarette and the present position is such that it is
not possible even for needy women and children to get sufficient food. Needless to say, therefore, at such inconvenient
places even our respectable Imperial Army is also not able to
get mosquito nets, foodstuffs, medicines and cigarettes. As
conditions are such, how can you expect me to treat you better than the Imperial Army? I do not prosecute according to
my own wishes and it is not due to the expense but due to the
shortage of materials at such difficult places. In spite of our
wishes to meet their requirements, I cannot do so with
money. I shall supply you, however, if I can do so with my
best efforts and I hope you will rely upon me and render your
wishes before me. We will build the railroad if we have to
built *[sic]* it over the white man's body. It gives me great pleasure to have a fast-moving defeated nation in my power. You
are merely rubble but I will not feel bad because it is [the fault
of] your rulers. If you want anything you will have to come
through me for same and there will be many of you who will
not see your homes again. Work cheerfully at my command.

(2)   I shall strictly manage all of your going out, coming back, meeting with friends, communications. Possessions of money shall be limited, living manners, deportment, salutation, and attitude shall be strictly according to the rules of the Nippon Army, because it is only possible to manage you all, who are merely rabble, by the order of military regulations. By this time I shall issue separate pamphlets of house rules of War prisoners and you are required to act strictly in accordance with these rules and you shall not infringe on them by any means.

(3)   My biggest requirement from you is escape. The rules of escape shall naturally be severe. This rule may be quite useless and only binding to some of the war prisoners, but it is most important for all of you in the management of the camp. You should, therefore, be contented accordingly. If there is a man here who has at least 1% of a chance of escape, we shall make him face the extreme penalty. If there is one foolish man who is trying to escape, he shall see big jungles toward the East which are impossible for communication. Towards the West he shall see boundless ocean and, above all, in the main points of the North, South, our Nippon Armies are guarding. You will easily understand the difficulty of complete escape. A few such cases of ill-omened matters which happened in Singapore [execution of over a thousand Chinese civilians] shall prove the above and you should not repeat such foolish things although it is a lost chance after great embarrassment.

(4)   Hereafter, I shall require all of you to work as nobody is permitted to do nothing and eat at the present. In addition, the Imperial Japanese have great work to promote at the places newly occupied by them, and this is an essential and important matter. At the time of such shortness of materials your lives are preserved by the military, and all of you must award them with your labor. By the hand of the Nippon Army Railway Construction Corps to connect Thailand and Burma, the work has started to the great interest of the world. There are deep jungles where no man ever came to clear them by cutting the trees. There are also countless difficulties and suf-

fering, but you shall have the honor to join in this great work
which was never done before, and you shall also do your best
effort. I shall investigate and check carefully about your coming back, attendance so that all of you except those who are
unable to work shall be taken out for labor. At the same time
I shall expect all of you to work earnestly and confidently
henceforth you shall be guided by this motto.

Y. Nagatomo
Lieutenant Colonel
Nippon Expeditionary Force

Chief No. 3 Branch
Thailand POW Administration

Appendix B

Unit	Last, First, Nickname	DATE	Place Of Death	Cause Of Death
N	ABRAMS, R. E	11/09/43	100 Kilo Camp, Burma	Beri Beri
N	ALDERMAN, H. P.	11/26/42	Aboard *Tofuka Maru*	Colitis
N	ALEVA, J. C.	06/24/44	Japanese Ship	Sunk En Route To Japan
H	ALEXANDER, J. G.	09/26/43	80 Kilo Camp, Burma	Tropical Ulcers
H	ANDERSON, J. A.	07/23/43	100 Kilo Camp, Burma	Beri Beri
N	ARMOUR, F.	07/17/43	100 Kilo Camp, Burma	Dysentery
N	BAERMAN, D.	09/27/43	80 Kilo Camp, Burma	Dysentery
F	BARNES Don H.	02/03/42	Aboard B-17, Camp Singasari, Malang, Java	Shot Down
N	BATCHELOR, W. C.	10/01/43	80 Kilo Camp, Burma	Tropical Ulcers
S	BAXTER, B. R.	09/13/43	80 Kilo Camp, Burma	Tropical Ulcers
N	BENDER, G. F.	05/22/44	Nakhom Pathom, Thailand	Dysentery
N	BENNER, C. W.	06/26/43	100 Kilo Camp, Burma	Dysentery
H	BINGHAM, J. E.	02/03/42	Aboard B-17, Camp Singasari, Malang, Java	Shot Down
N	BLAIR, K. S.	03/23/44	Kanchanaburi, Thailand	Beri Beri
DO	BOREN, Lemuel M.	08/01/43	80 Kilo Camp, Burma	Malaria
F	BOWEN, G. M.	12/11/43	105 Kilo Camp, Burma	Tropical Ulcers
D	BOWLEY, R. J.	01/23/44	Kanchanaburi, Thailand	Beri Beri
D	BOYLE, A. C.	11/16/43	80 Kilo Camp, Burma	Tropical Ulcers
N	BRANHAM, L. R.	08/17/43	100 Kilo Camp, Burma	Tropical Ulcers
S	BRAY, C. B.	09/18/43	100 Kilo Camp, Burma	Tropical Ulcers
N	BROTHERS, F. W.	11/08/43	114 Kilo Camp, Burma	Malaria
H	BROWN, J. R.	11/24/43	80 Kilo Camp, Burma	Dysentery & Tropical Ulcers
N	BUHLMAN, C. W.	09/06/43	80 Kilo Camp, Burma	Dysentery
N	BUSHNELL, E. W.	08/03/43	100 Kilo Camp, Burma	Tropical Ulcers

Unit	Last, First, Nickname	DATE	Place Of Death	Cause Of Death
H	BUSSEY, S. M.	01/09/44	Kanchanaburi, Thailand	Dysentery
N	CALLAHAN, M. C.	01/04/44	133 Kilo Camp, Burma	Tropical Ulcers
N	CANTRELL, J. A.	09/26/43	80 Kilo Camp, Burma	Tropical Ulcers
M	CARNEY, W. D.	07/22/43	100 Kilo Camp, Burma	Dysentery
N	CARTER, F. L.	09/14/43	80 Kilo Camp, Burma	Tropical Ulcers
H	COLLINS, C. M.	02/29/44	Kanchanaburi, Thailand	Dysentery
N	COOPER, D. R.	09/27/43	100 Kilo Camp, Burma	Tropical Ulcers
D	COX, C. A.	10/04/43	100 Kilo Camp, Burma	Dysentery
H	DEATS, L. F.	09/10/43	80 Kilo Camp, Burma	Tropical Ulcers
D	DELASIO, F.	12/23/43	Camp Nikki, Burma	Beri Beri
N	DEMOEN, A. R.	09/14/43	80 Kilo Camp, Burma	Tropical Ulcers
S	DEMPSEY, A. E.	08/20/43	100 Kilo Camp, Burma	Beri Beri
D	DICKENS, W. H.	01/01/44	114 Kilo Camp, Burma	Beri Beri
S	DOIRON, L. W.	08/29/43	100 Kilo Camp, Burma	Malaria
M	DRAKE, J. P.	08/01/43	80 Kilo Camp, Burma	Tropical Ulcers
MC	DUPLER, H. H.	05/14/43	Thanbyuzayat, Burma	Dysentery
F	EASTWOOD, H. W.	01/28/44	Tamarkan, Thailand	Malnutrition
N	EBAUGH, F. V.	09/14/43	100 Kilo Camp, Burma	Epilepsy
F	ECKLUND, R. L. "Swede"	01/05/44	103 Kilo Camp, Burma	Beri Beri
N	ELLIS, F. D	02/24/44	105 Kilo Camp, Burma	Dysentery & Malaria
N	FANCHOR, G.	12/19/42	Ohasi, Japan	Pneumonia & Diptheria
H	FAULKNER, G. F.	09/08/43	80 Kilo Camp, Burma	Tropical Ulcers
N	FEELEY, J. J.	11/28/43	80 Kilo Camp, Burma	Beri Beri
N	FELIX, I. A.	04/18/43	Batavia, Java	Tuberculosis
F	FORGEY, J. C.	09/27/43	100 Kilo Camp, Burma	Tropical Ulcers
N	GARWOOD, E. D.	09/09/43	80 Kilo Camp, Burma	Tropical Ulcers
D	GILLIAM, R. E.	09/23/43	100 Kilo Camp, Burma	Tropical Ulcers
H	GLATZERT, P. A.	06/24/44	Japanese Ship	Sunk En Route To Japan
N	GODFREY, D. F.	10/06/43	100 Kilo Camp, Burma	Dysentery
N	GRAHAM, R. G.	07/23/43	80 Kilo Camp, Burma	Tropical Ulcers
M	GRAY, H.	09/17/43	80 Kilo Camp, Burma	Dysentery
D	GRIFFIN, C. R	10/ /44	Batavia, Java	Dysentery
H	GUTHRIE, W. L.	09/10/43	100 Kilo Camp, Burma	Beri Beri
N	GUY, H. A.	08/12/43	100 Kilo Camp, Burma	Beri Beri
N	HALL, E. L.	10/02/43	100 Kilo Camp, Burma	Tropical Ulcers
H	HALL, H. L.	08/02/43	100 Kilo Camp, Burma	Dysentery
H	HAMMER, H. B.	06/24/44	Japanese Ship	Sunk En Route To Japan
DO	HAMPTON, R. W.	07/31/43	100 Kilo Camp, Burma	Dysentery
N	HANSEN, R. R.	08/23/43	80 Kilo Camp, Burma	Dysentery
D	HARRISON, J. W.	06/24/44	Japanese Ship	Sunk En Route To Japan
N	HATLEN, E. A	12/21/43	100 Kilo Camp, Burma	Beri Beri
E	HELEMAN, D. N.	/ /45	Japan	Beri Beri
N	HENDRICKS, R. H.	12/30/43	Kanchaniburi, Thailand	Dysentery
E	HERNANDEZ, A.	02/02/43	Surabaya, Java	Tuberculosis
H	HERRERA, L. M. "Lolo"	09/ /44	Nakhom Pathom, Thailand	Dysentery & Beri Beri
S	HICKS, J. W.	08/25/43	80 Kilo Camp, Burma	Tropical Ulcers
MC	HILL, D. W.	04/08/43	Serang, Java	Dysentery
N	HIRSCHBERG, L.	11/26/43	100 Kilo Camp, Burma	Tropical Ulcers
N	HITTLE, R. G	08/17/43	80 Kilo Camp, Burma	Tropical Ulcers
MC	HOLSINGER, F. O.	09/18/43	80 Kilo Camp, Burma	Tropical Ulcers

Unit	Last, First, Nickname	DATE	Place Of Death	Cause Of Death
N	HUTCHINGSON, B. M.	07/05/43	80 Kilo Camp, Burma	Dysentery
H	IVEY, D. B.	09/22/43	80 Kilo Camp, Burma	Tropical Ulcers
N	JAMES, E. R.	07/21/43	80 Kilo Camp, Burma	Dysentery
H	JASTER, A. H.	06/24/44	Japanese Ship	Sunk En Route To Japan
N	JOHNSON, E. I.	09/18/43	80 Kilo Camp, Burma	Tropical Ulcers
N	JOHNSON, H. M.	10/10/44	Borneo, N. E. I.	Tuberculosis
H	JONES, S. A.	09/11/43	80 Kilo Camp, Burma	Tropical Ulcers
M	JOWELL, J. D.	10/17/43	80 Kilo Camp, Burma	Tropical Ulcers
E	KALICH, N. O. F.	12/03/43	Japan	Spinal Meningitis
H	KALOUS, E. B.	09/06/43	100 Kilo Camp, Burma	Tropical Ulcers
S	KELM, A. M.	08/21/43	100 Kilo Camp, Burma	Dysentery
N	KETMAN, R. E.	09/05/43	100 Kilo Camp, Burma	Dysentery
H	KITCHINGS, H. A.	10/14/43	80 Kilo Camp, Burma	Tropical Ulcers
N	KOELLING, V. L.	09/11/43	80 Kilo Camp, Burma	Tropical Ulcers
N	KONDZELAL, F.	03/13/43	80 Kilo Camp, Burma	Malaria
N	KUNKE, C. J.	08/23/43	100 Kilo Camp, Burma	Tropical Ulcers
E	LAWSON, T. E.	06/24/44	Japanese Ship	Sunk En Route To Japan
N	LEE, E. H.	09/21/43	100 Kilo Camp, Burma	Beri Beri
N	LINDSLEY, A. J.	06/01/43	100 Kilo Camp, Burma	Dysentery
S	LOONEY, F. A.	06/24/44	Japanese Ship	Sunk En Route To Japan
MO	LUMPKIN, S. H.	08/01/43	100 Kilo Camp, Burma	Dysentery
F	LUNA, E.	09/22/43	100 Kilo Camp, Burma	Beri Beri
MC	LUSK, J. M.	03/22/43	80 Kilo Camp, Burma	Malaria
N	MANION, T.	08/23/43	100 Kilo Camp, Burma	Tropical Ulcers
F	MATTFELD, W. F.	11/16/43	114 Kilo Camp, Burma	Cardiac
E	McMAHAN, R. W.	06/24/44	Japanese Ship	Sunk En Route To Japan
F	MILLER, G. R. "Brodie"	09/18/44	Japanese Ship	Sunk En Route To Japan
H	MOORE, G. E.	10/ /43	Kanchanaburi, Thailand	Dysentery
D	MORRISON, C. D.	11/17/43	80 Kilo Camp, Burma	Tropical Ulcers
N	MUSTO, J. W.	07/17/43	39 Kilo Camp, Burma	Dysentery
D	OFFERLE, I. O.	11/18/43	80 Kilo Camp, Burma	Tropical Ulcers
N	OMOTH, R. E.	09/16/43	100 Kilo Camp, Burma	Cardiac
N	PARISH, B. H.	08/16/43	100 Kilo Camp, Burma	Beri Beri
M	PARKER, A. T.	11/17/43	80 Kilo Camp, Burma	Tropical Ulcers
N	PETERSON, L. O.	08/22/43	100 Kilo Camp, Burma	Dysentery
D	PFEIL, S. A.	08/22/43	39 Kilo Camp, Burma	Dysentery
N	PISTOLE, F. L.	12/26/43	105 Kilo Camp, Burma	Beri Beri
D	PITTS, G. E.	01/14/44	114 Kilo Camp, Burma	Beri Beri
N	PULLEN, R. H.	08/31/43	100 Kilo Camp, Burma	Tropical Ulcers
N	PYE, G. E.	08/13/43	100 Kilo Camp, Burma	Tropical Ulcers
S	REDWINE, A. L.	06/24/44	Japanese Ship	Sunk En Route To Japan
N	REED, C. O.	08/23/43	80 Kilo Camp, Burma	Dysentery
H	RHODES, B. E. "Dusty"	03/02/42	Bandoeng, Java	Gunshot Wound
H	RICH, R. L.	11/01/43	80 Kilo Camp, Burma	Beri Beri
F	ROGERS, J. W.	01/28/44	Tamarkan, Thailand	Dysentery
NO	ROSS, R. B.	05/05/42	Batavia, Java	Dysentery
N	ROSZELL, L. T.	08/05/43	Tarsoa, Thailand	Dysentery
N	ROTH, J. T.	08/05/43	100 Kilo Camp, Burma	Dysentery
D	RUSSELL, C. E.	09/07/43	100 Kilo Camp, Burma	Tropical Ulcers
D	SALAZMAN, M. F.	06/24/44	Japanese Ship	Sunk En Route To Japan
H	SCHANDUA, J. E.	09/14/43	100 Kilo Camp, Burma	Tropical Ulcers
N	SCHUELKE, J. H.	01/12/44	Kanchanaburi, Thailand	Dysentery

Unit	Last, First, Nickname	DATE	Place Of Death	Cause Of Death
S	SCHULTZ, L. D.	06/24/44	Japanese Ship	Sunk En Route To Japan
N	SEIDEL, A. G.	12/19/42	Ohasi, Japan	Bronchitis
F	SEWELL, D. H.	09/20/43	80 Kilo Camp, Burma	Tropical Ulcers
D	SEWELL, H. T.	06/24/44	Japanese Ship	Sunk En Route To Japan
D	SHAVER, H. D.	09/06/43	100 Kilo Camp, Burma	Dysentery
H	SHAW, E. E.	08/25/43	100 Kilo Camp, Burma	Tropical Ulcers
H	SILVA, E. J.	08/03/43	100 Kilo Camp, Burma	Dysentery
F	SIMPSON, Ward H.	01/30/44	Kanchanaburi, Thailand	Tuberculosis
S	SOKOLOWSKI, J. R.	09/18/44	Japanese Ship	Sunk En Route To Japan
N	SOULE, I. G.	09/09/43	80 Kilo Camp, Burma	Dysentery
F	SPARKMAN, L. S.	06/24/44	Japanese Ship	Sunk En Route To Japan
N	SPENCER, M. D.	11/09/43	80 Kilo Camp, Burma	Dysentery
E	STAVER, L. P.	05/23/45	Singapore	Cancer
H	STOUT, G. W.	10/31/43	80 Kilo Camp, Burma	Tropical Ulcers
N	TANBERG, A. N.	11/02/44	Saigon, F.I.C.	Dysentery
E	THOMAS, B.	10/27/43	Kanchanaburi, Thailand	Beri Beri
S	TIEMAN, E. W.	12/14/43	100 Kilo Camp, Burma	Beri Beri
S	TREMONTE, T. J.	07/29/43	100 Kilo Camp, Burma	Tropical Ulcers
N	TRIM, D. P.	12/11/43	105 Kilo Camp, Burma	Tropical Ulcers
N	TUCKER, W. E.	08/09/43	80 Kilo Camp, Burma	Tropical Ulcers
H	UPPERMAN, M.	10/04/43	100 Kilo Camp, Burma	Dysentery
N	WARD, F. C.	09/21/43	100 Kilo Camp, Burma	Tropical Ulcers
S	WATERS, N. H.	09/02/43	80 Kilo Camp, Burma	Tropical Ulcers
NO	WEILER, F. B.	03/26/42	Pandeglang, Java	Combat Wounds
S	WHATLEY, S. J.	08/25/43	100 Kilo Camp, Burma	Tropical Ulcers
N	WHITE, J. H.	03/13/43	80 Kilo Camp, Burma	Malaria
N	WIDMEYER, H. C.	09/10/43	80 Kilo Camp, Burma	Dysentery
N	WILLERTON, R. P.	06/24/44	Japanese Ship	Sunk En Route To Japan
N	WILLIAMS, D. M.	04/11/44	Tamarkan, Thailand	Dysentery
H	WILLIAMSON, B. R.	01/28/44	Tamarkan, Thailand	Dysentery & Malaria
N	WILLIS, D. W.	06/10/43	80 Kilo Camp, Burma	Dysentery
D	WILSON, E. P.	06/13/43	Tanbyuzayat, Burma	Allied Bombing
MC	WILSON, J. R.	10/ /43	114 Kilo Camp, Burma	Malaria
D	WILSON, T. A.	06/24/44	Japanese Ship	Sunk En Route To Japan
N	WINN, M. A.	09/19/43	100 Kilo Camp, Burma	Dysentery
E	WISMANN, E.	09/18/44	Japanese Ship	Sunk En Route To Japan
H	WOLTZ, D. G.	10/06/43	80 Kilo Camp, Burma	Malnutrition
N	YATES, D. R.	08/24/43	80 Kilo Camp, Burma	Beri Beri
S	YELL, A. B.	09/18/43	80 Kilo Camp, Burma	Dysentery
N	YOUNG, K. A.	12/22/43	100 Kilo Camp, Burma	Beri Beri

LEGEND

D   D Battery, 2d Battalion, 131st Field Artillery
E   E Battery, 2d Battalion, 131st Field Artillery
F   F Battery, 2d Battalion, 131st Field Artillery
H   Headquarters Battery, 2d Battalion, 131st Field Artillery
M   Medical Attachment, 2d Battalion, 131st Field Artillery
S   Service Battery, 2d Battalion, 131st Field Artillery
MC Marine Corps
N   U.S. Navy
O   Commissioned Officer

Bibliography

Bailey, Ronald H. *Prisoners of War.* Alexandria, Virginia: Time-Life Books, 1981.

Charles, H. Robert. *Last Man Out.* Austin, Texas: Eakin Press, 1988.

Fillmore, Clyde. *Prisoner of War.* Wichita Falls, Texas: Nortex Offset Publications, Inc., 1973.

Oda, Col. Akimitsu. *The Invasion of the Netherlands East Indies.* Tokyo, Japan: Headquarters, USAFFE and Eighth U.S. Army (Rear), 1958.

Ramsey, Winston G. *After the Battle No. 26, Death Railway.* London, England: Battle of Britain Prints International Ltd., 1979.

Sommers, Stan. *The Japanese Story.* Tampa, Florida: American Ex-Prisoners of War, Inc., 1979.

Teel, Horace G. *Our Days Were Years.* Quanah, Texas: Nortex Press, 1978.

Wigmore, Lionel. *The Japanese Thrust.* Canberra, Australia: Halstead Press, Sydney, 1957.

Special Consultation

Stanbrough, Jess H. Falmouth, Massachusetts, for advice on dates and locations of many events in this narrative.

Index

Shaw, M. Sgt. E. E., 47, 48
Sheppard Air Force Base, Texas, 126
Shintoism, 113
Singapore, 3, 23, 28, 54, 56, 57, 58,
   59, 60, 97, 98-101, 119, 132, 145
16th Japanese Army, 35
South China Sea, 54
Southeast Asia, 2, 3, 7, 29, 31, 46,
   106, 120, 128
Southern Army Railway Corps, 69
Southwest Conference, 137
speedo, 1, 5, 45, 59, 62, 80
Stanbrough, S. Sgt. Jess H., 10, 33,
   40, 48, 53, 121
Strabolgi, Lord, 36
Strait of Malacca, 3, 54, 63
Sunda Strait, 36, 45
Surabaya, Java, 24, 37
Sydney Daily Herald, 126

T
Tamarkan, 97, 98, 99, 100, 101, 103,
   106, 110-113, 115, 116, 126
Tanjong Priok, Java, 45
ter Poorten, Lt. Gen. H., 37
Thanbyuzayat, 1, 2, 54, 67, 68, 69,
   78, 143
Tharp, Lt. Col. Blutcher S., 4, 20,
   40, 42, 56
Theater Party, 99, 100, 101, 103,
   107, 109, 115
3d British Hussars, 35
3d Japanese Air Group, 35
3d Japanese Fleet, 35
36th Division, 1, 15
Thompson, James, 31
  Janis Kyle, 136
  Kay, 136

Linda, 136
tinko (count), 59, 105
Tojo, Gen. Hideki, 15, 131
torture, 116
Tower, Sen. John G., 109, 139, 141
Truman, Harry S., 111
23d Japanese Air Fleet, 36
2/3 Australian Machine Gun, 35
2/2 Australian Pioneers, 35

U
U.S. Veterans Administration, 133
United Press International, 136,
   137, 138, 139-141
USS *Houston*, 1, 36, 59, 73, 79, 95,
   133, 135, 147–150
USS *Pensacola*, 19, 21
USS *Republic*, 18, 19, 20, 21, 24

V
Varley, Brig. A. L., 56

W
Watergate, 141
Wavell, Field Marshal Earl, 28, 29,
   34, 37
Webb, Sgt. Wade H., 55
Wichita Falls, Texas, 7, 9, 10, 11, 14,
   51, 56, 90, 116-121, 123, 135,
   136, 139
Wigmore, Lionel, 35
Wisdom, Wiley, 11, 12, 13, 17
Woods Hole, Massachusetts, 121

Y
Yamashita, Lt. Gen. Tomoyuki, 28

Z
Zeigler, Capt. L. L., 121
Zero fighters, 30

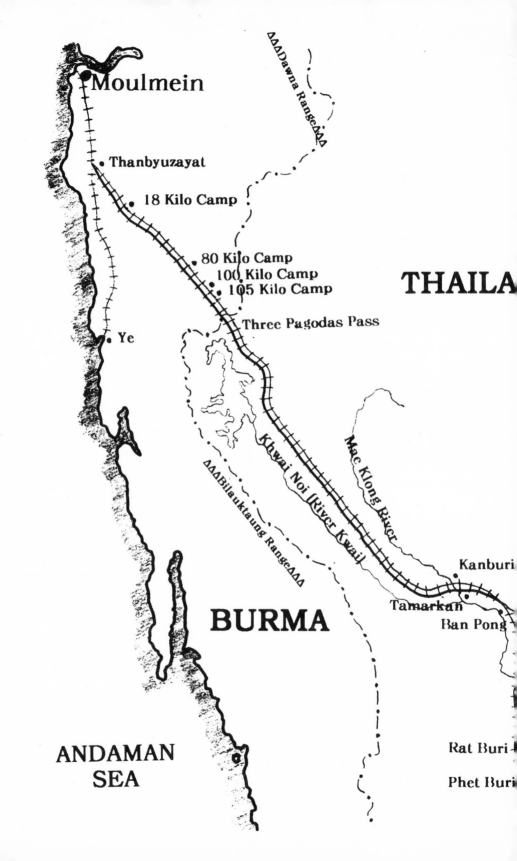